Supporting Children with Cerebral Palsy

Completely revised and fully updated in light of the 2014 SEND Code of Practice, this edition familiarises readers with the specific learning needs of cerebral palsy. Offering practical tips and tried-and-tested strategies from professional practitioners, this accessible guide provides advice on how to meet the needs of young people with cerebral palsy. This new edition presents all of the information practitioners will need to know to deliver outstanding provision for young people with cerebral palsy and support the inclusion of children and young people with cerebral palsy into main-stream schools.

The far-reaching advice found within this guide includes:

- Planning for a pupil with cerebral palsy
- Accessing the curriculum, including specific advice on each subject area
- How to make effective use of support staff
- Developing independence skills
- Liaising between home and school
- Making the transition into adulthood

With accessible materials, such as checklists, templates and photocopiable resources, this up-to-date guide will enable teachers and other professionals to feel more confident and effective in the support they can provide.

Rob Grayson – Team Leader for the Integrated Physical and Sensory Services, Hull City Council, UK.

Jillian Wing – Senior Support Teacher for the Integrated Physical and Sensory Services, Hull City Council, UK.

Hannah Tusiine – Senior Support Teacher for the Integrated Physical and Sensory Services, Hull City Council, UK.

Graeme Oxtoby – Senior Moving and Handling Adviser, Hull City Council, UK.

Lee Astle – Team Leader for the Integrated Physical and Sensory Services, Hull City Council, UK.

Elizabeth Morling – Series Editor, SEN Consultant and former Head of the Education Service for Physical Disability, Hull City Council, UK.

nasen
Helping Everyone Achieve ■■■

nasen is a professional membership association that supports all those who work with or care for children and young people with special and additional educational needs. Members include teachers, teaching assistants, support workers, other educationalists, students and parents.

nasen supports its members through policy documents, journals, its magazine *Special*, publications, professional development courses, regional networks and newsletters. Its website contains more current information such as responses to government consultations. **nasen's** published documents are held in very high regard both in the UK and internationally.

Other titles published in association with the National Association for Special Educational Needs (nasen):

Developing Memory Skills in the Primary Classroom: A complete programme for all
Gill Davies
2015/pb: 978-1-138-89262-0

Language for Learning in the Primary School: A practical guide for supporting pupils with language and communication difficulties across the curriculum, 2ed
Sue Hayden and Emma Jordan
2015/pb: 978-1-138-89862-2

Supporting Children with Autistic Spectrum Disorders, 2ed
Elizabeth Morling and Colleen O'Connell
2016/pb: 978-1-138-85514-4

Understanding and Supporting Pupils with Moderate Learning Difficulties in the Secondary School: A practical guide
Rachael Hayes and Pippa Whittaker
2016/pb: 978-1-138-01910-2

Assessing Children with Specific Learning Difficulties: A teacher's practical guide
Gavin Reid, Gad Elbeheri and John Everatt
2016/pb: 978-0-415-67027-2

Supporting Children with Down's Syndrome, 2ed
Lisa Bentley, Ruth Dance, Elizabeth Morling, Susan Miller and Susan Wong
2016/pb: 978-1-138-91485-8

Provision Mapping and the SEND Code of Practice: Making it work in primary, secondary and special schools, 2ed
Anne Massey
2016/pb: 978-1-138-90707-2

Supporting Children with Medical Conditions, 2ed
Susan Coulter, Lesley Kynman, Elizabeth Morling, Francesca Murray, Jill Wing and Rob Grayson
2016/pb: 978-1-138-91491-9

Achieving Outstanding Classroom Support in Your Secondary School: Tried and tested strategies for teachers and SENCOs
Jill Morgan, Cheryl Jones and Sioned Booth-Coates
2016/pb: 978-1-138-83373-9

Supporting Children with Sensory Impairment
Gill Blairmires, Cath Coupland, Tracey Galbraith, Elizabeth Morling, Jon Parker, Annette Parr, Fiona Simpson and Paul Thornton
2016/pb: 978-1-138-91919-8

The SENCO Survial Guide, 2ed
Sylvia Edwards
2016/pb: 978-1-138-93126-8

Dyslexia and Early Childhood
Barbara Pavey
2016/pb: 978-0-415-73652-7

Supporting Children with Dyslexia, 2ed
Hilary Bohl and Sue Hoult
2016/pb: 978-1-138-18561-6

More Trouble with Maths: A teacher's complete guide to identifying and diagnosing mathematical difficulties, 2ed
Steve Chinn
2016/pb: 978-1-138-18750-4

Supporting Children with Cerebral Palsy, 2ed
Rob Grayson, Jillian Wing, Hannah Tusiine, Graeme Oxtoby and Elizabeth Morling
2017/pb: 978-1-138-18742-9

Supporting Children with Behaviour Issues in the Classroom, 2ed
Sarah Carr, Susan Coulter, Elizabeth Morling and Hannah Smith
2017/pb: 978-1-138-67385-4

Supporting Children with Cerebral Palsy

Second Edition

**Rob Grayson, Jillian Wing,
Hannah Tusiine, Graeme Oxtoby,
Lee Astle and Elizabeth Morling**

Routledge
Taylor & Francis Group

LONDON AND NEW YORK

nasen

Helping Everyone Achieve

Second edition published 2017
by Routledge
2 Park Square, Milton Park, Abingdon, Oxon OX14 4RN

and by Routledge
711 Third Avenue, New York, NY 10017

*Routledge is an imprint of the Taylor & Francis Group,
an informa business*

© 2017 R. Grayson, J. Wing, H. Tusiine, G. Oxtoby, L. Astle & E. Morling

First edition published by David Fulton Publishers 2004

British Library Cataloguing in Publication Data
A catalogue record for this book is available from the British Library

Library of Congress Cataloging in Publication Data
A catalog record for this book has been requested

ISBN: 978-1-138-18741-2 (hbk)
ISBN: 978-1-138-18742-9 (pbk)
ISBN: 978-1-315-64316-8 (ebk)

Typeset in Helvetica
by Cenveo Publisher Services

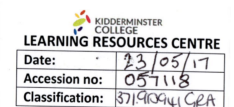

Contents

Foreword

This book was initially written by Jenny Fisher, Elizabeth Morling and Francesca Murray.

It has been rewritten to encompass new Government legislation and current practices in education by:

- Rob Grayson: Team Leader, Integrated Physical and Sensory Services (Hull)
- Jillian Wing: Senior Support Teacher Integrated Physical and Sensory Services (Hull)
- Hannah Tusiine: Senior Support Teacher Integrated Physical and Sensory Services (Hull)
- Graeme Oxtoby: Senior Moving and Handling Adviser (Hull)
- Elizabeth Morling, formerly Head of Service Education Service for Physical Disability
- With contributions from Susan Coulter: former Special School Headteacher

The authors named above have many years of experience of supporting children with physical disabilities and their families and the staff in the schools they attend, a large part of the authors' case load being pupils with cerebral palsy. The book is intended to support the inclusion of children and young people with cerebral palsy in mainstream settings.

A child with cerebral palsy is no different to any other child in that they will have individual personalities and individual strengths and needs. This publication is intended to give Special Educational Needs Co-ordinators, classroom teachers and teaching assistants comprehensive information and strategies that will enable them to fully support the pupil to reduce barriers to his/her learning and allow them to reach their potential. It is also essential that the views of the pupils and their parents are taken into consideration.

Contained within the book

- the legislation that empowers the pupil with cerebral palsy;
- planning for access;
- an overview of cerebral palsy and the characteristics that may impact on learning;
- suggestions and strategies to enhance learning, support assessment and develop planning;
- considerations for support staff;
- issues for pupils and parents;
- moving to adulthood;

- Continuing Professional Development (CPD);
- pro formas for access audits, Personal Evacuation Plans, Individual Health Care Plans, Intimate Care Plans.

The word school is mainly used throughout the book but this is intended to cover a variety of settings; nurseries, pre-schools and academies. Various terms are used within the book to refer to the individual with cerebral palsy, i.e. child, pupil or children and young people.

Section 1
Legislation and guidance

1 Legislation and guidance

The majority of pupils with cerebral palsy are educated in their local school or academy. Their condition is such that they can access the full curriculum when consideration is given to their learning, physical and emotional needs. However, a small number of pupils with significant needs may be educated in a special school environment.

Pupils with a physical disability (and possibly a learning need) are supported by the following legislation.

The Special Educational Needs and Disability Code of Practice, 2014 states that:

> All schools have duties under the Equality Act 2010 towards individual disabled children and young people. They must make reasonable adjustments, including the provision of auxiliary aids and services for disabled children, to prevent them being put at a substantial disadvantage. These duties are anticipatory – they require thought to be given in advance to what disabled children and young people might require and what adjustments might need to be made to prevent that disadvantage. Schools also have wider duties to prevent discrimination, to promote equality of opportunity and to foster good relations.

Definition of disability under the Equality Act, 2010

A person is defined as being disabled if they have a physical or mental impairment that has a 'substantial' and 'long-term' negative effect on their ability to do normal daily activities.

Disability rights

It is against the law for a school or other education provider to treat disabled pupils/students unfavourably. This includes:

- 'direct discrimination', e.g. refusing admission to a pupil because of a disability;
- 'indirect discrimination';
- 'discrimination arising from a disability', e.g. preventing a pupil from taking part in a school visit because of their disability;
- 'harassment', e.g. addressing a student inappropriately because they have not understood an instruction due to their disability;
- 'victimisation', suspending a disabled pupil because they have complained about harassment.

Reasonable adjustments

An educational provider has a duty to make 'reasonable adjustments' to ensure that disabled students are not discriminated against. These changes could include:

- **changes to physical features:** installing ramps to allow access to the building, classrooms;
- **providing extra support and aids:** specialist teaching and/or equipment, e.g. appropriate seating, ICT equipment.

The Special Educational Needs and Disability Code of Practice, 2014 states that:

> If children and young people with SEN or disabilities are to achieve their ambitions and the best possible educational and other outcomes … local education, health and social care services should work together to ensure they get the right support.

Some pupils may also have a medical need: 'The individual health care plan should be linked to or become part of the statement or EHC plan' (**Supporting pupils with a medical condition in schools, 2014**).

In order to ensure that pupils with cerebral palsy are able to access the curriculum without barriers to learning **The Teachers standards, Department of Education 2012** ensures that teachers must fully meet the needs of all pupils through the following standards:

A teacher must:

- Set goals that stretch and challenge pupils of all backgrounds, abilities and dispositions.
- Adapt teaching to respond to the strengths and needs of all pupils.
- Know when and how to differentiate appropriately, using approaches which enable pupils to be taught effectively.
- Have a clear understanding of the needs of all pupils, including those with special educational needs; those of high ability; those with special educational needs; those with English as an additional language; those with disabilities; and be able to use and evaluate distinctive teaching approaches to engage and support them.
- Make accurate and productive use of assessment
  - know and understand how to assess the relevant subject and curriculum areas, including statutory assessments.
- Fulfil wider professional responsibilities
  - deploy support staff effectively
  - communicate effectively with parents with regard to pupil's achievements and wellbeing.

The quality of teaching for pupils with SEN, and the progress made by pupils, should be a core part of the school's performance management arrangements and its approach to professional development for all teaching and support staff (Special Needs and Disability Code of Practice, 2014).

For pupils with medical needs, the document **Supporting pupils at school with medical conditions, 2014** gives comprehensive statutory guidance and non-statutory advice.

2 Moving and handling in the workplace

Some pupils with cerebral palsy require procedures involving moving and handling, e.g. the use of a hoist and a sling during toileting routines. It is essential that schools meet with legal regulations to ensure the safety of their staff and the pupil.

The main pieces of legislation relating to load management are:

- **The Health and Safety at Work Act (HASAWA) 1974**
- **Manual Handling Operations Regulations (MHORegs) 1992**

Employers' responsibilities

Employers have a duty to 'ensure so far as reasonably practicable the health and safety at work of all their employees' (https://worksmart.org.uk). In order to comply with the act they must provide the following:

- a safe working environment (rooms and equipment);
- information, training, instruction and supervision – ensure staff are aware of instructions provided by manufacturers and suppliers of equipment;
- a written health and safety policy/risk assessment;
- provision and maintenance of safety equipment and safe systems of work;
- systems to look after the health and safety of others, for example, the public and communicate with their health and safety representatives.

Employees' responsibilities

In order to comply with the act they must do the following:

- take care of their own health and safety and that of other persons (employees may be liable);
- co-operate with the employer to enable him to comply with his/her duties;
- use equipment correctly and appropriately and implement the training the employer has provided;
- use safe systems of work.

The Manual Handling Operations Regulations (MHORegs) 1992 places responsibilities on the employer for:

- avoidance of manual handling if at all possible;
- assessment of risks;
- reduction of risks;

- provision of information on the load (the client);
- review of risk assessments.

The aim is to reduce the level of risk to the lowest level reasonably practicable, therefore:

- use equipment and other aids to reduce risk;
- use safe systems of work.

The reporting of injuries

The legal requirement for reporting injuries is contained in the Reporting of Injuries, Diseases and Dangerous Occurrences Regulations (RIDDOR) 1995.

Employers must:

- report all specified incidents, accidents, and injuries to the appropriate outside agency;
- provide accident books in order to report accidents or incidents;
- communicate with health and safety representatives and inspect documents relating to accidents.

Employees must:

- report all accidents and injuries to the employer as soon as possible;
- ensure all accidents and injuries, are correctly recorded in the accident book.

COSHH

This will apply to the chemicals used for cleaning equipment. The legal responsibilities regarding exposure to hazardous substances are mainly covered within the Control of Substances Hazardous to Health Regulations (COSHH).

Employers must:

- carry out assessments with regard to health risks;
- prevent or control exposure to substances hazardous to health;
- ensure control measures and equipment are correctly used, maintained and in working order;
- monitor employees' exposure to any hazardous substances;
- provide appropriate health surveillance;
- provide suitable and appropriate information, instruction and training to employees as required.

Employees must:

- co-operate with their employers in the pursuit of compliance with COSHH and report any defects with equipment or measures;
- participate fully in health checks if required.

Lifting Operations and Lifting Equipment Regulations (LOLER 1998)

This is aimed at ensuring all lifting operations are properly planned, lifting equipment is used in a safe manner and that where necessary 'it is thoroughly examined at suitable intervals by a competent person' (https://worksmart.org.uk). A 'lifting operation' is lifting or lowering a load and applies to equipment that lifts or lowers as its principal function. This therefore applies to hoists.

Thorough examination is required:

- on initial use or following installations to ensure it is safe to use (i.e. hoists);
- periodically during its life, i.e. every six months or less if the equipment is for lifting people;
- following certain exceptional circumstances.

A 'competent person' may be the local authority (LA) Specialist Teaching Service for Physical Disability Service moving and handling specialist. He/she should be able to assess the safety of the lifting equipment and report back, in a written form, to the employer. A hoist will be stamped with the date when it was last inspected.

Slings should be inspected by the user, e.g. the teaching assistant who has been appropriately trained by a moving and handling specialist to check for wear, deterioration or damage.

It is essential that a person who carries out manual handling is aware that they can be held personally and legally accountable for their actions or inactions.

Provision and Use of Work Equipment Regulations 1998 (PUWER 1998)

Where equipment is **not** defined as lifting equipment, if it is used at work the provisions of PUWER will still apply:

- it should be suitable for the intended use;
- it should be safe for use, maintained in a safe condition and, in certain circumstances, inspected to ensure this remains the case;
- used only by people who have received adequate information, instruction and training;
- accompanied by suitable safety measures, e.g. protective devices, markings and warning.

Section 2

A profile of cerebral palsy and its impact on learning

3 What is cerebral palsy?

Cerebral palsy is a condition that affects muscle control and movement. It is usually caused by an injury to the brain before, during or after birth. Children with cerebral palsy have difficulties in controlling muscles and movements as they grow and develop. It can affect all muscle groups in their body.

There is no cure for cerebral palsy, but physical management can often help maximise and maintain physical skills. No two people will be affected by their cerebral palsy in the same way, and it is important to ensure interventions are tailored to the child's individual needs.

How common is cerebral palsy?

In the UK, cerebral palsy affects about one in every 400 children. Cerebral palsy can affect people from all social backgrounds and ethnic groups.

What causes cerebral palsy?

The main causes of cerebral palsy include:

- infection in the early part of pregnancy;
- lack of oxygen to the brain;
- abnormal brain development;
- a genetic link (though this is quite rare).

What can increase the chances of cerebral palsy?

The following factors can increase the likelihood of cerebral palsy:

- a difficult or premature birth;
- twins or a multiple birth;
- being the first child or fifth (or more) child;
- a baby of low birth weight (less than 2.5 pounds);
- a premature birth (less than 37 weeks).

A combination of the above (such as low birth weight and being a twin) can further increase the probability of cerebral palsy.

What are the types of cerebral palsy?

There are three main types of cerebral palsy. Many people will have a mixture of these types.

Spastic cerebral palsy

This type is present in around 75–88% of people with cerebral palsy; spasticity means the muscle tone is tight and stiff causing a decreased range of movement. As the muscle tone is so tight, spasticity can be very painful with muscles often going into spasm. It can affect many different areas of the body.

Dyskinetic cerebral palsy

This is sometimes referred to as dystonic, athetoid or choreoathetoid cerebral palsy. It is present in about 15% of people with cerebral palsy. Dyskinetic cerebral palsy causes uncontrolled, involuntary, sustained or intermittent muscle contractions as the muscle tone changes from tight to loose, often accompanied with slow, rhythmic movements. The whole body can be affected, which can make it difficult to maintain an upright position. Speech can also be affected as the person may experience difficulty in controlling the tongue, vocal chords and breathing.

Ataxic cerebral palsy

Ataxia is defined as an inability to activate the correct pattern of muscles during movement. Balance is affected and the person may have poor spatial awareness or find it difficult to judge their body position in relation to things around them. It's present in about 4% of people with cerebral palsy and can affect the whole body. Most people with ataxic cerebral palsy can walk but they will be unsteady with shaky movements. Speech and language can also be affected.

Mixed cerebral palsy

Many people with cerebral palsy will have a combination of the above types.

The following terms refer to the part of the body affected by the cerebral palsy:

- **hemiplegia** means that the person is affected on one side of the body;
- **diplegia** is where two limbs are affected;
- **monoplegia** is where one limb is affected;
- **quadriplegia** affects all four limbs.

Cerebral palsy affects mobility, co-ordination and any combination of the following:

- learning (many people with cerebral palsy have average and above average intelligence even when the level of physical disability is severe);
- hearing (around 8% of children are affected);
- vision;
- visual perception;
- sleep patterns;

- communication;
- eating and drinking, including swallowing and chewing problems and difficulty manipulating cutlery and dishes;
- toileting, including bladder and bowel control;
- attention and concentration.

There may be associated medical conditions, e.g. epilepsy (up to a third of children with cerebral palsy).

Does cerebral palsy change?

Cerebral palsy itself is not progressive; the injury to the brain does not change. However, the effects may change over time for better or worse.

For further information refer to SCOPE (www.scope.org.uk).

4 What does cerebral palsy mean for a child?

Some or all of the following may apply to the pupil with cerebral palsy

restricted mobility – poor balance, use of a wheelchair, sticks, walking frame;

physiotherapy input – specialist equipment such as the above plus possibly a standing frame; a physical management programme;

occupational therapy input, including developing functional skills, assessment for specialist seating, specialist toileting equipment;

communication difficulties – slow processing of instructions, questions, difficulty with articulation, hard to understand, input from the speech and language therapist;

limited attention – easily distracted;

communication aids;

hearing or vision problems;

visual perception difficulties impacting on many areas of school life;

medical issues, e.g. epilepsy;

need for a differentiated curriculum;

restricted fine motor skills;

use of ICT equipment;

difficulties with dressing;

need for support for toileting with specialist equipment;

physical restrictions restricting peer interaction;

possible low self esteem;

resilience and persistence.

---

5 Two case studies

The following case studies reflect the wide variations of impact the condition can have on a child.

Lucy

Lucy is a four-year-old girl in the Foundation Stage of a large mainstream primary school. She has a left-sided hemiplegia, which causes her to have restricted use of her left hand and slight difficulties with her left leg. She is a very determined little girl whose parents have encouraged her to be as independent as possible.

She is working at age appropriate levels in all areas. She understands and follows all the directions within the classroom, processes language and responds appropriately and understands all the concepts being explored within the early years curriculum. She can use a pencil to write her name (although somewhat awkwardly) and draw age appropriate pictures of herself. She needs reminding to use her right hand to secure her work and also when carrying out two-handed activities such as riding a bike or pushing a doll's pram.

She takes part in all outdoor activities with enjoyment. She has input from the paediatric physiotherapist and has to wear a splint on her left leg to aid balance. She also has exercises from the same source to maintain the range of movement in her left hand.

She uses the toilet (grab bars were fitted to aid stability) with independence, can wash both hands and dry them. She needs a little help with dressing. She can eat a cooked lunch with independence.

Alfie

Alfie is in Year 6 and has quadriplegic cerebral palsy. He is a popular boy within his class. He is working towards level 3 in all subjects. He finds it extremely difficult to use a pencil so he has access to ICT to record in all subjects. Some of his ideas are scribed for him. He has good understanding of language but takes time to process and respond. His answers are age appropriate.

He has an electric wheelchair for all mobility in and out of school. He has a high level of input from a paediatric physiotherapist who then trains the teaching assistant to carry out his physical management programme. This involves an exercise programme that is carried out on a daily basis. He also has a standing frame that he has to use for half an hour a day. He does long sitting (sitting with legs outstretched) for half an hour a day. The class teacher and physiotherapist liaise in order to plan the best times to implement the physical management, e.g. the standing frame is used for guided reading and the long sitting for class discussions. The transfers from place to place are essential for his long-term well being. Alfie takes part in PE lessons using his wheelchair and enjoys being out at playtime to join in the football games. He is part of a wheelchair football team as an out-of-school activity.

Alfie requires adult support (again with guidance from the physiotherapist and a LA Moving and a Handling Adviser) to use the toilet. As with many boys with cerebral palsy he chooses to use the toilet as little as possible at school. The procedure involves using a hoist and sling to move him from the wheelchair to the toilet. He can put on his hat and scarf but requires support for dressing. He can eat a packed lunch with some independence but finds it difficult to manipulate cutlery and requires help to eat a cooked lunch.

The following chapters include the characteristics of cerebral palsy that impact on the pupil's access to learning.

6 Mobility

The range of mobility of pupils with cerebral palsy varies greatly but is the area that has the greatest impact on a pupil. Some pupils will have little or no problems with mobility while others will need assistive devices. These can be walkers of varying types, sticks or orthotics that aid balance. Other pupils, whose mobility is more severely impaired, will require the use of a wheelchair to get from one point to another. Some pupils will require support to move their wheelchair; others will be able to self-propel their chair. Electric wheelchairs give pupils the maximum amount of independence to move around school or away from home. Some pupils will have surgical interventions that improve balance or correct gait.

Increasing mobility as far as possible has health benefits such as improving muscle strength and dexterity to bone and skin health as well as stimulating the appetite and improving circulation, and intestinal tracts. It is therefore important that pupils have opportunities for mobility as frequently as possible, even if it is only from wheelchair to classroom seating. Input from a physiotherapist is essential to maximise a child's physical potential and well being and it is essential that schools implement the advice given. This will include a physical management programme and possibly the use of specialist equipment.

Some pupils enjoy taking part in wheelchair sports, including basketball and football. Accessible bikes are also available in some localities, which allow children to take exercise and have fun with their families. All terrain wheelchairs allow access to more difficult outdoor environments.

7 Vision

It is thought that 40–75% of children with cerebral palsy have a visual problem or impairment (www.tbvi.edu/seehear).

This can include:

- **acuity loss** typically makes things blurry, which can be improved through the use of spectacles (therefore it is important that the pupil wears them);
- **field loss** means that part of the field of vision (the ability to see about 180 degrees in all directions when looking straight ahead) is missing;
- **oculomotor problems** can affect depth perception and smooth movement of the eye;
- **visual concentration;** pupils with cerebral palsy have such problems overcoming other difficulties, e.g. balance when concentrating on visual tasks.

8 Visual perception

Children with cerebral palsy may have difficulty with visual perception, i.e. difficulty interpreting and making sense of the visual information they receive.

The Test of Visual Perception (TVPS) breaks visual perception into six discrete areas. The areas are described below together with possible difficulties. *Ideas to help overcome these difficulties are written in italics.*

Visual discrimination

This is the ability to distinguish similarities and differences between shapes and objects and it is a pre-requisite for developing other visual perception skills.

Difficulties could be:

- confusion with similar shapes, objects, letters, words, numbers or pictures: try *sorting trays*;
- lack of observational skills: try *finding objects/people from a description, 'Where's Wally?' books*;
- difficulties with 'odd man out' activities: try *odd one out games with objects then pictures, such as 'what's wrong' and 'what's missing' pictures.*

Visual memory and sequential visual memory

This includes short-term memory, which is the working memory and long-term memory that is essential for recognising and categorising shapes and objects and organising new information.

Sequential visual memory is essential for following written instructions, reading and ordering letters when spelling.

Difficulties could be:

- remembering letter shapes, numbers and words: try *games (pelmanism, Kim's game), verbalise information, multi-sensory approach to letter writing, apps;*
- learning spellings: word patterns and shapes, try *sequencing activities, mnemonics, computer games, e.g. 'Nessy';*
- organisational skills: *use desk prompts, lists, settings on phones that give reminders.*

Visual spatial relationships

This is the understanding of how objects relate to themselves and to each other. As a child moves its body within a space and interacts with its environment it learns to relate to other objects around them and how they relate to each other. Obviously a pupil with cerebral palsy with limited mobility has less ability to explore their environment.

Difficulties could be:

- orientating letters/numbers correctly: try *multi-sensory activities to develop correct formation (making letter patterns/letters with wet paint brushes, in sand, on whiteboards), apps, desk prompts*;
- understanding of directional words and prepositions: try *positional games with the pupil, small world toys*;
- lack of body awareness: try *games to name body parts, develop awareness of space around by reaching for objects with eye closed/throwing bean bags into a bucket*;
- getting lost and being unsure of which way to go: try *a buddy system, maps with colour coding for different subject areas in school*;
- negotiating through obstacles: try *obstacle courses, remote control vehicles*;
- placing letters on a line: *work on letter placement, particularly ascenders and descenders, bold lines, line guide and writing frames*;
- laying out work correctly: try *left to right activities, examples of what the work should look like, dot at the beginning of the line to signify where to start*;
- ordering letters correctly in word: *spell the word using magnetic letters when given it in writing*;
- correctly spacing words: try *finger spacers, child editing a part of their work (e.g. marking with a highlighter pen where a space should be)*.

Visual form constancy

This is the ability to recognise a shape or object whatever its changes in context, size orientation, size or colour.

Difficulties could be:

- in recognising similar shapes in different orientations: try *using a multi sensory approach tracing with the finger, looking for matching shapes around the classroom*;
- confusing letter shapes, faulty letter formation, learning to write cursive script; try *multi-sensory approach to developing letter formation, use simple joined hand-writing scheme*;
- in recognising letters if the font is changed: try *offering work with letters/words in different fonts, e.g. letters of their name*;
- recognising partly hidden objects in reality or pictures, e.g. not being able to name a picture because it is partly covered or not recognising a hockey stick when the bottom half is hidden by the storage basket: *play games to reveal letters/numbers that have been partly hidden and the child reads them (gradually increase the amount hidden)*.

Visual figure ground

This is focusing attention on an object and separating it from its background.

Difficulties could be:

- distraction by visual stimuli, movement in the room, colourful wall displays with difficulty returning to a task without prompting: try *seating in front of and facing the teacher in the most distraction free part of the room, keeping the working area free from clutter*;
- negotiating objects on the floor: *encourage peers to keep the floor tidy and give an easy walk way to the pupils seat*;
- working on a 'cluttered worksheet: *use pastel coloured paper or whiteboards and keep information and illustrations to the minimum, use larger, simple font*;
- cutting out shapes because it is hard to distinguish between the outline and the background: *use a bold outline with one picture to a sheet (ensure the appropriate scissors are available)*;
- skipping or repeating words when reading: *use a reading ruler, create sentences on Clicker that can be read back, highlight mistakes*;
- judging the speed of an object, e.g. ball or a car, coming towards them: *reminders of where to look and focus attention, use of brightly coloured balls to show up against a background*;
- being unable to find objects/pictures amongst a clutter: *teach methodical searching (e.g. left to right, top to bottom using a finger to guide the eye), store equipment in clearly marked storage, allow time to clear up.*

Visual closure

This is recognising a shape when it is shown in an incomplete form.

Difficulties could be:

- inability to recognise partly hidden objects: *play games to reveal letters/numbers that have been partly hidden and the child reads them (gradually increase the amount hidden)*;
- faulty letter formation, developing joined script: *as for visual form constancy, use of ICT for recording work.*

The following are general considerations to be made to overcome visual perception difficulties:

- build up simple routines;
- tidy a work area before the start of a new task;
- mark an area of personal workspace for a pupil to have boundaries within which to work, without spreading into his/her neighbour's space;
- use cards with cues (visual or written) to help the organisation of a task;
- use cues (visual or written) to help structure the timetable for a whole or part of a day;

- keep articles required for different subjects in transparent wallets to facilitate clear identification;
- have storage areas in the classroom clearly labelled with a picture and/or written label to aid the collection and storage of equipment;
- provide support for new pupils to a school (buddy system) to enable the pupil to familiarise him/herself with the new layout of the building or site;
- use a diary to enable the pupil to organise him/herself for PE, homework;
- use a visual guide when reading, e.g. a piece of card, finger;
- support the development of dressing skills by encouraging the pupil to lay out his/her clothes neatly, put them in a pile in the order which they were removed and have clothes with logos, etc. to identify the back/front, use picture cues to give the order of dressing;
- give information in small sections (one instruction at a time with a gradual build up);
- give pupils opportunities to talk through activities;
- avoid placing pupils next to distractions, e.g. windows, a busy corridor, a bright display;
- create worksheets with a minimum of information and avoid distracting detail.

For further information see LOOK, SEE ..... KNOW and UNDERSTAND (ReLEASE booklets available from IPaSS 01482 318400).

9 Communication

Communication is vitally important. It allows us to express our needs and feelings, build relationships and explain ourselves. Some children with cerebral palsy may have little difficulty with communication, while others may have problems in a large variety of ways:

- articulating particular speech sounds;
- an inability to produce coherent speech;
- the ability to understand what is said to them (receptive language) but be unable to respond appropriately;
- being slow to process receptive language.

Some pupils may require alternatives to verbal communication, i.e. Augmentative and Alternative Communication (AAC), a blanket term used to describe methods of communication that do not involve direct speech. Advice regarding AAC is available from the pupil's specialist speech and language therapist and/or local authority specialist teacher.

The following may be considered:

- sign language, e.g. Makaton, which will be developed from a very early age;
- symbols;
- a communication passport that introduces the child to everyone they meet and tells them about their needs and ways they communicate;
- switches that can be set to give simple responses such as 'yes' or 'no';
- high-tech options such as 'Liberator' and 'Proloquo2go', which turn symbols and text into speech at the touch of a button.

There are ways to support the pupil's communication. The following will need to be considered in relation to the pupil's level of development.

- Seek advice from the speech and language therapist. Ensure their programmes are implemented by appropriately trained staff.
- Communication aides should be available at all times.
- Most importantly, ask the pupil's views at all times rather than taking the 'Does he take sugar attitude' and automatically doing things for them.
- When children are very young, begin practising how to give information about themselves, e.g. 'My name is Jenny Smith.' Move on to cover the address, birth

date, age, school, likes and dislikes. The pupil must learn to communicate key information about themselves without the support of an adult.

- Play games where the pupil has to listen out for and follow increasing numbers of key words (information-carrying words). 'Can you wash baby's hands?' where there is a choice between a baby and teddy, wash cloth and hairbrush.
- Ensure the pupil has to ask for things. Use carrier sentences to support requesting and other interaction: 'Can I have…?' 'I want…' 'Can I play?'
- Teach the whole class to use 'Makaton' (or the mode of signing used). Ensure staff are trained to develop this skill.
- Sound buttons (easily found on the Internet) can have a message recorded on it, e.g. 'I would like a hot dinner', to allow a child to give a response to a question.
- Give the pupil's first name, pause and ensure their attention before speaking.
- Encourage face-to-face interaction with good eye contact.
- Use simple, familiar language and short concise sentences, in the order events will happen, e.g. 'put your coat on, go out to play'.
- Make books that practise functional language that the child might want to use in other contexts, e.g. 'I like' book or 'My favourite things'.
- Use visual timetables, both individual and class.
- Give pupils questions at an appropriate level and give them adequate time to respond, to demonstrate that the answers are valued. The teacher could try counting to 10 to allow the pupil time to respond before repeating the question and encouraging a response. This is a good strategy to use with all children and to encourage them to practise amongst themselves.
- Use sign, pictures, objects, interactive whiteboard and tablets to make all teacher input more accessible and memorable. Record ideas on small whiteboard or ICT, ready for later use.
- Encourage the pupil to speak aloud by using visual and written prompts. The pupil may find it easier to read information than to speak spontaneously.
- Set up regular and additional opportunities to speak to others, e.g. taking and reading messages.
- Develop expressive opportunities through puppet and small world play, drama and role play.
- Use a home-school diary (book, sound button, iPad) to prompt the pupil with restricted communication skills to share his or her news with parents and help adults and peers understand what the pupil is saying – ideally supported by a photo. Parents can then write in return about something the pupil has done in the home context, including photos or relevant objects from a visit. The pupil must be given the opportunity to share this within the classroom, preferably within their peer group. The app 'Special Stories' facilitates this with ease and allows the child to record themselves reading the sentence without the pressure of an audience. Clicker Stories is also useful for longer pieces.

10   Developing concentration

Pupils with cerebral palsy may have difficulty developing concentration skills. The following table shows the stages of development and gives strategies to improve the skill.

Stages of development	Activities to develop concentration
Stage one This is the stage of extreme distractibility. The pupil's attention moves from one object or event to another.	Provide toys to catch the pupil's interest – windmills, bouncing toys, bubbles, squeaky toys, roller ball tracks. Use toys with which the pupil can easily create a reaction. Use toys that require the pupil to follow e.g. a large, noisy car. Rhymes – 'Round and round the garden.'
Stage two The child can concentrate for some time on a concrete task of their own choice. The pupil may not tolerate any intervention in the task in hand and can be very single channelled.	Demonstration by an adult of a toy, allow the pupil to play, extend the pupil's exploration and vocalise action, e.g. posting boxes, building towers of bricks and knocking them down, water play. Use of cause and effect computer programs and cause and effect switched toys. The completion of the tasks makes the reward part of the activity, e.g. form boards.
Stage three Attention is still single channelled but becomes more flexible. The pupil's full attention must be on the directions and immediately transferred to the task. The directions may be verbal or the task may be demonstrated.	Gain attention before giving short instructions. Short tasks with reward given for completion of the task. Give adult support for the task to avoid frustration developing. Matching games, copying patterns with crayons, simple jigsaws, picture books, nesting boxes.
Stage four The pupil has to alternate his full attention between the speaker and the task but he/she does it without the adult needing to focus his attention.	Aim to reduce adult input. Encourage attention to task by comments, e.g. 'Well done'. Encourage the pupil to stay on task while listening to the instruction. Build up concentration from a one-to-one situation to larger groups.

Stages of development	Activities to develop concentration
Stage five The pupil can assimilate verbal directions without the need to interrupt the task. Pupils at this stage are ready to be taught in a class, where directions are often given to the class while the pupils carry out a task.	The pupil should concentrate with minimal input, i.e. occasional prompts if attention lapses. The pupil should be able to work alongside others.
Stage six This is the mature school level. Integrated attention is well established and well sustained.	The pupil can be introduced to more complex stimuli.

NB The above stages illustrate a normal progression of the stages of concentration. Some pupils will require very structured objectives to achieve progress. Movement from one stage to another may be a very slow process. It is important that the pupil's ability to learn independently is incorporated in the pupil's IEP. Ensure that the objects and tasks are age appropriate.

11 Developing listening skills

Some pupils with cerebral palsy may have difficulty developing listening skills. The stages of development are linked to the stages in 'Developing concentration'.

Stage 1 The pupil is extremely distractible. Appropriate activities would be:

- Encourage attention to sounds using activity toys that make noises – rattles, musical toys, jack-in-the-box, wind chimes, spinning tops.
- Sing rhymes to the pupil.

Stage 2 The pupil is learning to tolerate the adult's presence and involvement in an activity of the pupil's choosing. Appropriate activities would be:

- Encourage attention to sounds with the use of activity toys that make noises – cars with sound effects.
- Use musical instruments – draw attention to the different sounds.
- Use action rhymes – 'Ring a roses'.
- Make a choice of two activities – 'Do you want to paint or do a jigsaw?'
- Ask the pupil to fetch familiar objects – 'Find your coat', etc.

Stage 3 The pupil is beginning to control his/her focus of attention. Suitable activities would be:

- Ask for objects, e.g. 'Show me the lion', using miniature toys or pictures.
- Sing nursery rhymes and songs and leave a pause for the child to supply the missing word. Play musical statues.
- Read familiar stories, with repetitive lines for the child to join in, e.g. The Three Little Pigs.
- Read a story on an individual basis. Ask the pupil to hold up a toy animal when he/she hears the name of the animal in the story.

Stage 4 The pupil is beginning to transfer attention skills to the group. Suitable activities would be:

- Match sounds to objects or pictures.
- Tell a story with a child's name in it. Ask the pupil to put his/her hand up when he/she hears their name.

- Ask for objects, build up the number of objects in the sequence, e.g. put objects in a shopping bag.
- Follow simple commands – ask the pupil to touch two or three body parts.

Stage 5 The pupil is transferring attention to the classroom situation. Suggestions for activities:

- Play Simple Simon Says.
- Read a story. Give the pupils pictures to hold up when they hear the name of the article on the picture.
- The pupils sit in a circle. When a name is called, the bean bag is thrown to that pupil.

12 Hearing difficulties

It is thought that 13% of pupils with cerebral palsy have some sort of hearing impairment, with 3% having a more severe loss. The following strategies should support hearing difficulties:

- Seek advice from the hearing impairment service, if appropriate.
- Place the pupil near the front of the class (within the limitations of the pupil's mobility).
- Gain the pupil's attention before speaking.
- Face the pupil when speaking to him/her.
- Avoid standing in front of the window when speaking to the pupil.
- Reinforce speech with signs, gestures and encouragement to watch other pupils.
- Support phonic knowledge with a pictorial scheme (e.g. 'Jolly Phonics') and give other prompts – pictures, prompts in a written form.
- Play sound bag games to encourage auditory discrimination skills where the pupil has to sort objects into sets according to two given sounds.
- Use short listening activities/games to strengthen auditory skills.
- Repeat other pupils' responses.
- Repeat instructions to the pupil after the whole group input, to ensure understanding.
- Have an environment that is as free from auditory distraction as possible.

13 Medical issues

Some pupils with cerebral palsy may have additional medical needs, including epilepsy. The document **Supporting pupils at school with medical conditions, 2014,** DfE gives comprehensive statutory guidance and non-statutory advice for governing bodies in order for schools to fully meet the needs of pupils with a medical condition.

The document should be referred to in order to gain more detailed information. Some pertinent issues are:

- Individual Health Care Plans (IHCP) will be essential to ensure the medical needs of the pupil are met. It should be devised by the relevant health care professional, e.g. specialist paediatric epilepsy nurse in conjunction with the SENCo and parents. A template can be found in the appendix.
- School staff who are required to administer medication or carry out procedures related to a specific condition, e.g. catheterisation, should receive sufficient and suitable training and achieve the necessary level of competency before they take on the responsibility. The relevant health care professional should normally lead on identifying and agreeing with the school, the type and level of training required, and how this can be achieved. A registered healthcare professional must administer training; parents or another member of staff are not sufficient.
- Several members of staff should receive the above training in case of staff absence.
- Administering medicines is not part of teachers' professional duties, however, they should take into account the needs of pupils with medical conditions that they teach, i.e. the medical needs, the educational implications and social and emotional aspects of the pupil.
- Administration of medication should be witnessed by another member of staff and recorded appropriately. This should show what, how and how much was administered, when and by whom. Any side effects of the medication to be administered at school should be noted.
- All medicines should be stored safely in an appropriate non-portable, lockable container. Only named staff should have access.
- Essential medication should be available when the pupil is off-site, e.g. on school trips. The IHCP should be adhered to and there should be some reference to school visits (including short off-site visits, e.g. swimming lessons) within it.

A template for an Individual Health Care Plan can be found in the appendix.

Section 3
Planning for the pupil

14 Transition from one setting/school to another

In order to ensure a smooth transfer a number of considerations need to be made, as the pupil makes the transition from one setting to another, be it from pre-school to primary school or primary to secondary school. However, all the following points may not need to be acted upon, this will depend upon the severity of the pupil's condition.

The considerations should include:

- A carefully prepared transition plan, which is drawn up at the Education Health Care Plan meeting, held in the final year of the early years setting or the primary school. This should involve information from:
    - the teachers, SENCOs and support assistants from the early years setting, primary school and the secondary school;
    - professionals from outside agencies, e.g. educational psychologists, speech and language therapists, specialist teaching service for physical disability, occupational therapists and physiotherapists;
    - parents;
    - the pupil.

The plan should consider:

- visits from the receiving school staff to the pupil in their current setting to discover the strengths of the pupil, their needs and successful strategies currently in place;
- additional visits to the receiving school for the pupil;
- home/school communication;
- management of support; on transitions around school, in the learning environment and at non-structured times;
- access to the curriculum and how differentiation will take place;
- transfer of the pupil's learning profile, i.e. the levels of attainment, appropriate learning methods, language skills, areas of strength and difficulty;
- personal profile of the pupil with contributions from the primary school, parents and friends;
- the need for therapy programmes and suitable places for these to be delivered.

The considerations should also include:

- An access audit should be carried out in conjunction with the SENCo, site manager and the specialist service for pupils with a physical disability.

- Support for the pupil to learn new routines, the layout of the school and transition from one lesson to another. Maps could be compiled together with a walk around the building. Photographs or a video could be taken on pre-visits to be used for further preparation work, e.g. of the classrooms for various subjects and of key members of staff. IPads, smartphones or tablets are ideal for this.
- The pupil's 'One Page Profile' should be in place.
- Staff training should be put into place to give an overview of cerebral palsy and the individual needs of the pupil. This may be available from the Local Authority's Specialist Teaching Service for Physical Disability.
- The appropriate use of adult support (possibly more than one worker) should be discussed, in order to support subjects and promote independence. The individual capability of selected staff to undertake necessary tasks should be determined.
- Training for staff with regard to moving and handling and the correct use of equipment should be sought from the Local Authority Teaching Service for Physical Disability. The Health and Safety Act should be adhered to.
- A Personal Emergency Evacuation Plan (PEEP) should be put in place.
- Appropriate access to all parts of the school site should be determined for wheelchair users, with adult support where necessary.
- Consideration should be given to the ambulant pupil's stamina in a school on a large site – this may require support. This could include timetabling of tutorial groups in a ground floor room, use of lifts.
- Places to leave bags, PE equipment should be determined.
- A reduction in the timetable may be considered if a full one is too taxing.
- PE lessons will require adaptations and differentiation.
- Support maybe required for dressing after PE.
- Lunchtime may require planning, e.g. the pupil may find it easier to go into the dining area when it is quietest (with a friend), need support with making a choice and carrying food plus finding a place to sit with peers. Adapted feeding equipment may be required.
- Some pupils will be able use the toilet independently (perhaps using the accessible toilet). Others will require the support of an adult in the area with appropriate equipment. Appropriate staff should be allocated to facilitate the pupil's requirements. Staff must volunteer for certain roles, e.g. toileting. This requirement should be within the teaching assistants' job description.
- Appropriate seating may be required, the occupational therapist will advise.
- The pupil's means of communication should be acknowledged and guidance gained from the speech and language therapist.
- The pupil's method of recording work should be taken into consideration and relevant ICT equipment should be in place. There may be a need for a scribe for some pupils.
- Consideration should be given to organisation at unstructured times, e.g. break and lunchtimes.
- Peer group integration may require support through encouragement to join clubs, buddy systems, Circle of Friends.
- Development of understanding of the nature of cerebral palsy for peers could be delivered through PHSE lessons or assemblies (the parents' and pupil's views should be taken into consideration regarding the content of this).
- Medical conditions may require extra support outlined within an Individual Health Care Plan.

- Effective parent partnership is essential for the pupil to settle into a new school and good communication is important for joint strategies to take place. It should be acknowledged that all parents do not have the confidence to communicate easily with a secondary school and strategies will be required to overcome this, e.g. a member of staff from the primary school could accompany the parents on a school visit, having previously discussed any concerns of the parents. They may also support the parents in subsequent meetings. Support from a parent partnership organisation may also be provided.
- Consider how homework tasks are recorded, e.g. diary or electronically. Homework must be appropriate for individual pupils; the amount given may need to be reduced in quantity.

The above issues are addressed in the following chapters.

15   Access issues

In order to meet the physical needs of the pupil an access audit should be undertaken by the SENCo, site manager and a member of staff from the Local Authority Specialist Teaching Service for Physical Disability, the physiotherapist and occupational therapist, prior to the pupil starting school.

The audit should include the following (all of which will not be required, it will depend on the level of need of the pupil):

Arrival at school

- disabled parking;
- identification of entry and departure points;
- stairs, steps, slopes, door access, which may impede or aid access;
- local authority home-school transport service may be used and the pupil may need greeting on arrival.

On-site mobility

- minimise distances for transition around the site;
- the timetable may be altered to facilitate easier movement between lessons;
- timetable lessons on the ground floor where possible;
- oversight for change of lessons;
- break and lunchtime supervision.

Equipment required to give access to the site and the curriculum

- rollator, wheelchair (manual or electric), standing frame, specialist seating.

Movement of equipment

- identify who will move equipment;
- minimise the transitions required through careful planning;
- ensure safe moving and handling procedures take place.

Seating in the classroom and the assembly hall

- ensure classroom furniture is arranged to permit maximum access for pupils using aids for mobility such as sticks, wheelchairs, rollators;

– near the door to enable easy access in and out of the classroom; this is particularly useful if it is arranged for a pupil to leave some lessons early to avoid crowds when travelling between lessons and/or to carry out a physical management programme.

Equipment to access the curriculum

– ICT equipment may need to be set up, batteries will need re-charging and the pupil's work will require printing;
– specialist science and technology seating and equipment may be required.

At breaktimes

– provide the pupil with a 'buddy' to open doors, gain access to the toilet;
– be aware that static pupils become cold more quickly than those who are more mobile and will need appropriate clothing;
– have a quiet area for less active pupils to talk;
– provide alternative options at breaktime for a group of pupils, e.g. tabletop games;
– allow time for pupils using wheelchairs or mobility equipment to have as full a breaktime as possible, by letting them leave the classroom a few minutes early;
– have an adult-led game in the playground to include pupils who are unsteady or unsure.

Feeding

– access to the dining hall with suitable seating;
– appropriate feeding equipment;
– support for making food choices and carrying food.

Toileting

– an accessible toilet with an alarm, grab bars and space for wheelchair access;
– specialist equipment, i.e. hoist and sling plus a changing plinth may be required;
– physical management room with a hoist and changing plinth;
– advice and moving and handling training will be required from the OT and LA Specialist Teaching Service for Physical Disability Moving and Handling Adviser.

Medical needs

– an area for administering medication should be identified with an appropriate storage place for medication;
– sterile areas for procedures, e.g. catheterisation.

A 'Personal Emergency Evacuation Plan' (PEEP) should be in place to detail plans to evacuate disabled pupils in the event of an emergency.

A disabled pupil with mobility difficulties will require a 'Personal Emergency Evacuation Plan' (PEEP). This will detail plans to evacuate disabled pupils in the event of an emergency; this is particularly important if the school building contains more than one level (most lifts will not operate in the event of a fire alarm, so a contingency plan is required for when disabled pupils are taught on upper floors). See the Appendix for a pro forma.

The Fire Service has produced the 'Fire Safety Risk Assessment Supplementary Guide – Means of Escape for Disabled People' (2007), which contains all the information required to create a PEEP (www.gov.uk/government/uploads/system/uploads/attachment_data/file/422202/9446_Means_of_Escape_v2_.pdf).

16 Off-site activities

Governing bodies should ensure that their arrangements are clear and unambiguous about the need to support actively pupils with medical conditions to participate in school trips and visits, or in sporting activities, and not prevent them from doing so. Teachers should be aware of how a child's medical condition will impact on their participation, but there should be enough flexibility for all pupils to participate.
(Supporting pupils with a medical condition in school, 2014)

The following considerations should be made:

- A risk assessment should be carried out prior to *any* visit (however long its duration), so that planning arrangements can take place. The Health and Safety Executive (HSE) also gives guidance on school visits.
- Consultation should take place with parents and pupils to determine the level of support required for bathing, dressing and feeding.
- The staff of a site to be visited, e.g. leisure centre, residential setting should be informed of a pupil's condition to ensure the pupil is safe at all times.
- Suitable transport should be arranged that has appropriate access for a wheelchair user or a pupil with restricted mobility. The transport may also need to have the ability to carry extra equipment, e.g. hoist, walking frame, electric wheelchair etc.
- Access to the buildings at a residential setting or at places to be visited should be checked for suitability.
- Appropriate toileting facilities: an accessible space or a neighbouring school may offer a suitable facility, hoisting equipment. Provide for the pupil's intimate care needs, e.g. clean pads and disposal equipment plus staff requirements such as gloves, aprons. A RADAR key may be useful as this opens about 9000 accessible toilets. It costs about £5 and is available from Local Authorities or Disability Rights UK.
- More easily accessed toileting alternatives may be possible, e.g. urine bottles, 'shewee' (a bottle for female use www.shewee.com).
- If appropriate the Individual Health Care Plan (IHCP) should be taken, which will include emergency contact numbers of parents and local hospitals, medication.
- If medication is required plans should include:
  - storage, locked cabinet, fridge;
  - dosage;
  - trained person and witness for administration;
  - recording of medication given;
  - emergency medication.

- Guidance should be requested from parents to indicate the need for extra snacks, drinks or alternative diets.
- Accompanying staff who are trained to support the pupil's needs, e.g. the need for hoisting. For extended visits, staff will volunteer and cannot be coerced.
- The risk assessment will determine which activities are suitable for certain pupils and alternatives may be required.

Section 4

Meeting the educational needs of the pupil with cerebral palsy

17 Classroom management

Classroom planning

The following ideas should provide a good working environment for the pupil with cerebral palsy:

- Read all reports from outside agencies, which will help to determine specific needs of the pupil within the classroom.
- Seek advice from the Specialist Teaching Service for Physical Disability with regard to setting up the classroom and for relevant equipment to support the pupil.
- The pupil who uses a walking aid or wheelchair should be able to enter the classroom without furniture having to be moved and having a clear access route to their desk.
- Teach all pupils to place their chair under the table when they leave and to stow their bags under the table to allow the pupil with restricted mobility an easier passage through the room.
- Ensure the pupil can reach equipment when seated in his/her wheelchair. Provide an individual set of equipment for pupils with limited mobility so that they do not have to rely on help from others.
- Adaptations to the classroom environment may be needed to encourage independence, e.g. coat hooks that are easily reached and are away from the most crowded area, an easily accessed drawer/locker.
- The pupil must have a good sitting posture. The occupational therapist (OT) may give advice as specialist seating may be required. Encourage a whole class approach to monitoring pupil's sitting position. Aim for all children to sit with feet flat on the floor, bottom to the back of the chair, back straight, head in the middle. This will aid concentration and reduce fidgeting.

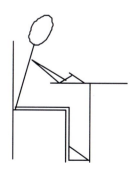

- Ensure furniture is at the correct height for the pupil, to allow concentration on the task rather than balancing. Provide appropriate sized tables, with chairs that allow the pupil to place their elbows comfortably on the table.
- Footblocks will allow their feet to rest on a surface and provide a comfortable working position.
- Some pupils with cerebral palsy might need a sloping writing surface to improve the working position. Consider the use of a commercial sloping board or an empty arch lever file. If the use of ICT is the main method of recording, the correct placing of this is important to allow for hand function and visual perception difficulties. The OT may offer advice.
- Ensure the pupil sits facing the teacher/whiteboard wherever possible to overcome any difficulties with visual perception or hearing.
- Place a pupil with weak visual skills in the middle towards the front of the classroom – reducing the angle of eye-to-board-to-book movements. Avoid placing them at the back as they will have too many interfering movements between them and the board.
- If the pupil has difficulty extracting information from the interactive board, try using different coloured fonts for each line, or writing key words in different colours, or format text into boxes so that the pupil knows which box he needs to give attention to.
- Consider using a visual timetable (a class or individual one) to encourage independence.
- Ensure specialist equipment, e.g. scissors, rulers etc., is easily accessed.
- Ensure all ICT equipment is available if required.

18 Differentiation

The Teachers Standards, Department of Education, 2012 states that a teacher must:

Set goals and standards that challenge pupils of all backgrounds, abilities and dispositions.

Adapt teaching to respond to the strengths and needs of all pupils

- Know when and how to differentiate appropriately, using approaches which enable pupils to be taught effectively. Materials should be adapted to meet the level of the learner.
- Have a clear understanding of the needs of the pupils, including those with special educational needs; those with high ability; those with English as an additional language; those with disabilities; and be able to use and evaluate distinctive teaching approaches to engage and support them.

Make accurate and productive use of assessment

- Know and understand how to assess the relevant subject and curriculum areas, including statutory assessments.

Pupils with cerebral palsy may have other areas of difficulty, such as learning difficulties, hearing and visual difficulties or speech and language difficulties. The level of effort demanded by a pupil with cerebral palsy to perform a function or carry out a task may be higher than that of their peers. Due to these issues they may become frustrated when working on activities within the classroom.

Differentiation is a way of ensuring that all pupils are given a chance to display knowledge, skills and attributes required by the curriculum. It is important for teachers to have a good understanding of what level the pupil is working at in order to set realistic and achievable targets. Understanding the capabilities as well as the limitations of a pupil with cerebral palsy will help them to succeed at school.

By differentiating learning opportunities the pupil will have the chance to develop their self-esteem, confidence, and enjoyment of learning. Providing positive feedback and giving pupils the opportunity to answer questions are examples of how this may be done.

Differentiation can take place in a number of ways:

General strategies

Gain a full picture of the pupil's needs, i.e. physical, emotional and learning, that are barriers to learning by talking to the SENCo, former teacher, parents and the pupil. The SENCo should have the information, which will be garnered from outside agencies and experience of school staff.

- Assessment will determine the level at which work will be set. The manner in which assessment should take place will vary according to the pupil's level of physical and cognitive ability. Some pupils will be working along national norms and others will require a more tailored approach (the chapter on 'Assessment' gives some ideas).
- Understand the capabilities and skills of the pupil on which to build. Realistic and achievable targets can then be set.
- Sharing planning (short, medium and long term) with teaching assistants will help them to better support the pupils they are working with and enable them to find/ prepare resources that may be useful. For example, a word bank can be created for software such as Clicker.
- The pupil is entitled to the same amount of teacher input as other pupils. It is not acceptable for the pupil's teaching assistant to be responsible for differentiating teaching for the pupil.
- Consider groupings to allow pupils with cerebral palsy to work individually, in pairs and in small groups.
- It is important to assess the pupil on the objective of the lesson. For example, in a science lesson focus on the scientific understanding of the pupil rather than the presentation of their work.
- Be sensitive by providing similar activities for the pupil that are not too different from their peers so their self confidence is not undermined.
- Pupils may benefit from a multi-sensory approach to learning. For example, when learning to form letters they could use sand, iPad apps, use playground chalks outside.

Specific teaching strategies

- Language used to give pupils instructions and information should be clear and concise without unnecessary small talk.
- Verbal 'teacher talk' introductions to lessons may need to be tailored to take into account the pupil's attention span.
- Pupils may benefit from pre-teaching of a subject to ensure a level of confidence before approaching new tasks.
- Regular assessment by the teacher of pupils' understanding on a 1:1 level will give the pupil the opportunity to share their views and clarify any misconceptions.
- Scaffolding tasks will give pupils a starting point, for example, using a storyboard to plan written work.
- Prepare templates on the pupil's laptop, e.g. the format of a letter so that they record the content of their letter.

- Put maths problems onto their laptop or in their book so that they only have to work out the answers.
- Give pupils questions at an appropriate level and give them adequate time to respond, to demonstrate that the answers are valued.
- Provide positive feedback.
- Use a wide range of assessment materials to ensure that the pupil's level of attainment is measured accurately.
- Tasks should be broken down into small steps with possible small breaks in between.
- Cue cards could be used to encourage pupils to collect the appropriate equipment needed for that lesson i.e. cue cards with a picture of a pen, ruler, calculator for maths.
- Prompt cards may also encourage independent working.
- It may be appropriate to record the date and learning objective for the pupil to give them more time to record their responses to the task.
- Ensure homework is recorded as necessary in the pupils' planner, home-school diary or by email. The homework set may not be identical to that of their peers due to the fact that it will take pupils with cerebral palsy longer to process and record information.
- The views of the pupil are also important; they may find it discouraging to see that they have a different worksheet or are using different equipment.

Recognise the level of effort demanded to enable a pupil to perform a function or carry out a task. The pupil will have to put in far more effort than their peers in order to complete a task.

Resources to support differentiation

- Resources from a lower key stage may be appropriate for some pupils.
- Written materials may be tailored to the individual pupil. For example, by considering the pupil's reading level, ensuring that information is in an appropriate sized print/font and presenting information that it is not visually cluttered. Images to support the text would be very helpful.
- Provide artefacts or pictures that enhance the topic, give a better understanding and also prompt ideas for writing.
- Provide a handout or PowerPoint presentation or write on a white board for a pupil to copy rather than expecting them to copy from an Interactive White Board.
- Pre-drawn diagrams will overcome drawing difficulties and allow the pupil to fill in the labels (either a paper copy or an electronic one).
- Supplying support staff with key vocabulary and subject specific language will prepare the pupil for new topics.
- Pupils may require specialist equipment to access lessons such as rulers, pens, pencils, writing slopes or larger equipment such as specialist seating. Small pieces of equipment may be organised together in a desk tidy/chair tidy.
- ICT equipment must always be available if this is the main method of recording work. Clicker grids should be prepared in advance. Maths work could be ready on the ICT equipment so that the pupil just has to work out the answers.

Awareness of time

- Tasks should be broken down into small steps with small breaks in between.
- Additional time should be allocated to complete tasks. This should not infringe upon the pupil's social time, i.e. break and lunch times.
- It may be necessary to alter the timetable to allow for 'catch up' time, if completing a task within a lesson becomes difficult.
- Alternatively, it may be relevant to reduce the amount of work expected within a lesson, e.g. the number of maths problems to be solved may be less, relative to their peers.
- Allow time for pupils to process information in order to answer questions or participate in discussions.
- The pupil may need additional time for organisation such as collecting equipment needed for the lesson.
- An element of the curriculum may be planned in order to allow for use of specialist equipment, e.g. reading when using a standing frame.
- Pupils may need additional time to move between classrooms or different parts of the school, e.g. they may need to leave lessons five minutes early to avoid busy corridors.

Exam access arrangements

Careful consideration of a pupil's needs for access arrangements in exams must be given well ahead of time. This could include additional time, provision of an amanuensis and use of ICT. Consult the current JCQ publications for further details of exam access arrangements. See the chapter 'Assessment'.

19 Mathematics

The following may be considered in order to meet the needs of the pupil:

- Small resources may be difficult to manipulate. Adaptations may be needed by using a larger resource or through adjustments using materials such as Dycem (non-slip material) or Velcro.
- Some pupils have significant difficulties handling standard number equipment, e.g. Unifix™ cubes. These invariably end up on the floor, or the pupil loses count and does not develop a reliable counting pattern. This is simplified by using an abacus or stringing cubes on a cord.
- Difficulties with visual perception can impact on a child's ability to visualise numbers. Use of Numicon can help:

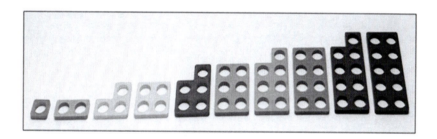

- Larger squared paper for recording work may be helpful.
- Use number stamps to record the answer to a number question if writing numbers is difficult.
- Explore the use of computer programs for maths to avoid problems with recording work.
- When pupils begin to use a calculator they may repeatedly hit the wrong number. A large-buttoned calculator solves this difficulty.
- A multifunction calculator can be found in the 'All Apps' menu within 'Windows 10' for those who need it.
- Non-slip rulers can be found in a number of education catalogues. 'Alligator easi grip' rulers are fun and easy to use.

- Standard classroom rulers can be made non-slip by the simple addition of two small strips of 'self-adhesive' Dycem™ placed on the underside. A coloured sticker in the middle of the ruler also prompts the child to place his or her fingers in the correct position to draw a line. Holding the ruler at one end only, usually results in the other end being pulled down by the pressure of the pencil as it is drawn along it.
- For those pupils who have difficulty using a standard compass, the best alternative is the safe drawing compass, circle protractor or circle scribe. These can be used to draw circles of different diameters; the safe drawing compass also measures angles.

20 Literacy

The following suggestions may support literacy lessons, it will be necessary to assess the pupil's level of development before implementing them.

- Ensure the task is within the pupil's level of understanding. Simplify the task if necessary.
- Follow up class input with individual input; use picture or written prompts.
- Check understanding of the task and content of the lesson.
- Use real objects or pictures printed from the class input as prompts to overcome difficulties and prompt language with work recorded in the following way:
  - pupil gives verbal sentence;
  - the adult scribes the sentence (typed or written);
  - the pupil then copies the sentence using an iPad, AlphaSmart.
- If news writing is required, ask the family for photographs, objects from weekend activities.
- Cut up sentences that match well-known stories, for pupils to sequence. The sequenced sentences could be stuck into the pupil's book and captions added if appropriate.
- Demonstrate what is required, e.g. the adult types a sentence and asks the pupil to follow, with a sentence of their own.
- Use iPads to recall events, e.g. school visits, prior to writing about the visit.
- Use photographs to write captions for.
- Use the Clicker program with grids made using vocabulary the pupil can read and linked to the subject being studied in the classroom.
- Have an individual alphabet chart/word book/dictionary on their table.
- Use computer programs for learning spelling, e.g. 'Nessy'.
- Use storyboards and picture sequences to provide ideas to write about.
- A writing frame can help with organising thoughts and the writing process itself. There are a number of software titles that may support this. Mind-mapping software can help to quickly get a number of ideas down quickly without worrying about structure or order.
- If necessary, suggest choices of sentences, characters, settings or activities for characters.
- Make use of visual prompts to aid writing skills, e.g. a defined area to write in, a red dot where the writing is to start.
- It is essential that the reading level of the pupil is taken into consideration. Ensure the correct font size is used in books and on worksheets.

- Appropriate recording methods will need to be assessed. Various alternative methods are described in the following chapters.
- Time should be given to respond to questions during discussions.
- Consider whether it is appropriate or not to ask a pupil with speech difficulties to read out loud during guided reading time.

21 Physical education

Just like the majority of their peers, pupils with cerebral palsy (CP) are often enthusiastic about participating in PE lessons; lessons provide a break from the classroom, opportunities for fun and friendship and the chance to explore their physical capabilities.

Unlike the majority of their peers, however, there may be barriers that affect their participation:

- Many pupils with cerebral palsy follow a Physical Management Programme (PMP) designed by their physiotherapist to support mobility and postural needs. With the demands of the National Curriculum and to maintain opportunities for socialisation at break and lunch times, some pupils may miss some or all of their PE lessons to follow their PMP. If this is the case, liaise with the physiotherapist to see if PMP exercises can be incorporated into the warm-up element of lessons and encourage participation in as many aspects of the lessons that time and best practices for safety allow.
- Pupils with severe cerebral palsy may have considerable co-ordination difficulties that make it very difficult for them to participate in PE activities. Some will have equipment to support their mobility, e.g. walking sticks, walking frame, manual or powered wheelchair; this equipment will affect their capacity to participate, may be a risk to their and their peers' safety and must be factored in to planning.
- Pupils with cerebral palsy may have associated difficulties with vision or hearing that can affect their participation. If this is the case, make sure that you position yourself close to the pupil and make time to work individually with them to enhance learning.
- Pupils with cerebral palsy may find it difficult to concentrate on whole class skills teaching elements; if this is the case, ensure that support staff are in a position to model the skills after teacher input and make time to work individually with the pupil to enhance learning.

Communication is vital for working successfully with any young person with a disability:

- Find out about the individual and not just the disability – cerebral palsy is a complex condition affecting all individuals differently; get to know the young person, find out how interested they are about sport, how confident they are physically and what they feel they are capable of doing independently before assigning support.

- Liaise closely with the young person's physiotherapist to seek their advice in terms of limitations to participation, activities deemed inappropriate from a medical perspective and support regarding the minimisation of risk.
- Speak to the SENCo for any other information that may be helpful for inclusion planning.

Emphasise ability rather than disability by placing disabled pupils at the centre of planning; plan lessons around their abilities rather than trying to 'fit them in' to a mainstream lesson.

Although this may appear daunting initially, getting it right can be very rewarding – for the teacher, the disabled pupil and their peers!

There are a number of excellent resources available online to support planning:

TOP Sportsability

Website: www.topsportsability.co.uk.

This is an excellent online resource for schools and offers practical advice to teachers, learning support staff, and other sports practitioners.

It consists of video clips and downloadable content showing ideas and strategies around the inclusion of young disabled people in physical activity and is divided into four resources:

- **User manual** – Introduces TOP Sportsability and provides a user guide to the resource and overviews of models of inclusion; for instance, their STEP model provides a basic framework for adapting any PE activity for inclusion:

  S – Space – Change the space in which the activity is taking place – make the space bigger, smaller or create zones to assist inclusion; T – Task – Change the nature of the activity to ensure all can be involved; E – Equipment – Change the type, size or colour of equipment used to aid inclusion; P – People – Change the people, e.g. the numbers in teams and/or ways in which they are involved, and how they interact with each other.

- **Disability sports** – Introduces a range of disability sports and adapted games with sports-specific resources.
- **Sports adaptations** – Provides suggestions and resources to help practitioners adapt a range of more traditional or mainstream sports.
- **Wheelchair skills** – An introduction to basic wheelchair movement skills and how this knowledge can be transferred across a range of sports-specific wheelchair-based activities.

The English Federation of Disability Sport

Website: www.efds.co.uk

This website details the work of the charity, including its support to national governing bodies to help them be more inclusive and organise disability sports events around the country.

There is a link to the Sainsbury's Active Kids for All Inclusive PE Training Programme, which offers free training to school staff and other sports practitioners to develop inclusive PE, sport and physical activity for disabled people. The training is backed up by an online resource to support continued professional development and to enable good practice to be shared. Staff training in developing the fitness of disabled pupils is also available through the charity's 'Inclusive Fitness Initiative' (IFI) programme.

The Inclusion Club

Website: www.theinclusionclub.com

This site has lots of videos, tips, resources and other information derived from all over the world. It is possible to sign up to access all of the information and receive a monthly update.

The Sports Coach UK

Website: www.sportscoachuk.org

This site has lots of information relating to inclusive coaching practices. A selection of excellent resources include Impairment Specific Coaching Awareness factsheets, general inclusion advice and sports specific information, including 'Kicking up a Racket', a Badminton England Coaching Resource to support inclusion in this sport.

In addition to lessons, an Inclusive Sports Club could be set up at lunchtimes or after school. This could be an ideal opportunity to introduce inclusive sports such as boccia, table cricket or goalball to pupils. All that is needed to get started, including information, resources and equipment, can be found using the websites above.

22 Accessing the technology curriculum

All pupils should be included in technology lessons regardless of their skill level. Some may question the value of 'supported practical work'. D&T is a valuable subject that teaches an understanding of the how the world works. It also enables pupils to plan and evaluate the practical work carried out under their direction, an essential life skill for some people with cerebral palsy.

The following points may support teachers planning for differentiating Design and Technology and the curriculum to include pupils with cerebral palsy:

Select finely graded specific objectives:

- to be able to select equipment for measuring and marking wood;
- to be able to give accurate instructions to the adult helper to facilitate cutting wood.

Consider deployment of support staff for each activity:

- support staff to work with an individual pupil or a small group of pupils;
- support staff to modify/enlarge/simplify class work sheets.

Agree recording strategies with support staff, which will inform assessment of pupils' work:

- brief written notes by the support assistant can enable teachers to have an accurate record of support given in each lesson.

Ensure all practical work is pupil led:

- when support staff are assisting with practical tasks the support assistant must work under the direction of the pupil (except when to do so would be dangerous).

Assess work using the same criteria as for other pupils:

- if a pupil has given correct instructions to their support assistant then credit them for their knowledge and understanding.

Consider classroom organisation and equipment storage:

- a wheelchair user will require a workbench of an appropriate height;
- an individual tool set will minimise movement within the classroom;
- make other pupils aware of safety implications of a pupil working in a wheelchair; the wheelchair user is vulnerable at this height.

Consider special arrangements for examinations:

- pupils with additional physical needs are entitled to have the same assistance in examinations as they have in lessons;
- these arrangements can include a practical assistant, additional time, use of an amanuensis, rest periods and separate facilities;
- further details are available from individual examination boards on the QCA website and 'GCSE examinations. Implications for candidates with cerebral palsy and associated disabilities.' Scope Advisory Assessment Service (updated annually).

Consider working out of key stage:

- pupils may work from the programmes of study of a lower key stage to enable them to progress and demonstrate achievement;
- work should be presented in a context suitable to a pupil's age.

Some adapted equipment may be required

Technology

Request advice from the occupational therapy service or LA specialist teaching physical disability service regarding use of standard equipment and specialist equipment.	
Ensure at least one set of equipment is stored at an accessible height.	
	Provide a perching stool if the pupil is standing for prolonged periods or if balance is a problem. (https://www.nrshealthcare.co.uk)
	Pupils who have good use of one hand can use an auto chopper instead of a knife to chop vegetables.

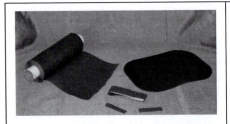	Damp tea towels can help to stabilise a mixing bowl. Dycem™ Non-slip mats are useful for anchoring a range of equipment. They are available in two thicknesses. Thick mats are useful for trays, chopping boards and heavy mixing bowls. The thin variety is supplied on a roll and can be cut to size.
	A knob turner can be used for turning taps or knobs on a cooker. It comprises a series of retractable metal pins that mould to the shape of the object, providing a firm grip. This would be useful for pupils who have limited hand strength or reduced grip due to arthritis.
	The sandwich spreader board hooks over the edge of the table and enables pupils to spread bread using one hand.
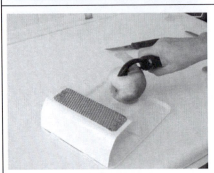	Vegetable holding boards are available that incorporate a grater and spikes to hold a vegetable whilst peeling it.
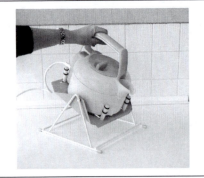	A kettle tilt can be used to ensure safe pouring of hot liquids. They are available in a variety of shapes and can be used to hold jugs and teapots. A useful safety tip: encourage pupils who have tremors to stand their receptacle on a tray; if there are any spills it won't go on the floor.

A panhandle holder allows pupils to stir without holding the panhandle.

- Use electrical equipment that duplicates a manual function, e.g. food processor for chopping vegetables, rubbing in method for pastry, creaming sugar and fat for cakes.
- Use a mounting system for hand-held electrical tools. These may need to be designed and made by a D&T technician.
- Use commercially available clamps to stabilise work when marking and cutting.
- Provide an individual set of tools, possibly lightweight or junior versions, to be used by pupils with low muscle tone or weakness in their hands.

Higher cost adaptations

- Pull-out storage racks in cupboards are easy to access.
- An adapted height adjustable work station should be available in all schools, including hob and sink to provide access for all pupils.
- Spaces should be available under worktops to allow access for wheelchairs.

If these facilities are not in place it should be included in the school's accessibility plan.

Ovens

- A wall-mounted built-in oven with pull-out tray and slide and hide door will protect the wheelchair user's legs.
- A combination microwave oven on an accessible work space would negate the need for an oven.

Textiles

Craft activities tend to rely on being able to use both hands at the same time. Stabilise work using Blu-Tack, Dycem™, clamps.

- provide large bodkins (metal or plastic) with bigger mesh materials.

An appropriate sewing machine may need to be considered, e.g. one that uses hand function alone rather than a foot treadle.

23 Science

The guidance at the beginning of the 'Accessing the technology curriculum' chapter will also apply to practical elements of science lessons. Some specialist equipment may be useful. The Local Authority Specialist Teaching Service for Physical Disability will be able to advise on specialist equipment for practical subjects. The following could also be considered:

- Specialist seating may be appropriate (advice may be given by the occupational therapist).
- It will be necessary to find a bench that allows a wheelchair user to work.
- Risk assessments may be needed before experiments are carried out.
- Use appropriate equipment, e.g. unbreakable test tubes and beakers with non-slip matting, where possible.

24 Art

Some children with cerebral palsy may have missed pre-writing developmental activities due to a focus on developing their gross motor movement. Children will try to find a comfortable and stable position for drawing. This might be sitting, standing or lying. Generally, short and fat equipment, i.e. chunky pencils and crayons, are easier to use than long and thin implements.

Younger children	Older pupils
Try: • chunky chalks/pastels; • thicker and shorter-handled paint brushes, including shaving brushes/decorating brushes; • working at an easel or an adjustable-angled table may be easier to use for a wheelchair user; • 'T-bar' brush holders; • non-tip paint pots/holders; • using clips/Dycem™ to keep work in place; • printing with stamps rather than painting.	• Art/CAD apps to support design aspects; • use 'clip art'/scanned images to support art modules; • stabilise paper with clips or Blu-Tack; • use non-slip matting to secure equipment; • place paint pots in holders; • ensure the appropriate specialist scissors are available; • ensure correct seating is used; stools may compromise balance (seek advice).

25 ICT

The use of ICT may be beneficial to pupils with cerebral palsy who are having difficulties recording work by hand. Using ICT can help pupils by:

- enabling access to the curriculum where they may otherwise have difficulty demonstrating their learning;
- increasing the volume of work they are able to record;
- increasing speed with recording work;
- improving the presentation of work;
- developing confidence and independence within the classroom.

There is a wide variety of ICT equipment used to record work available. This could include desktops, laptops, iPads, Neos, AlphaSmarts or Touch Screen monitors. For pupils with visual difficulties the use of a non-glare screen may be beneficial.

Hardware refers to the physical parts that make up a computer. Pupils with cerebral palsy may require inclusive hardware such as adapted keyboards or controls in order to benefit from the opportunities for learning that ICT holds. Some examples are described below:

Keyboards

Equipment	How could this help a pupil with cerebral palsy?	What might it look like?
Large keyboard e.g. 'Big Keys Keyboard'	Larger keys are more easily targeted by pupils who experience difficulties with fine motor control. Some keyboards may be colour coded to highlight vowels/consonants or can be purchased with lower case letters. The keys can be arranged in an 'ABC' format rather than the standard 'QWERTY'.	Inclusive Technology Ltd

Hand held keyboards e.g. XEBEC Tech	Can enable children with limited movements to strike appropriate keys as the small-size keyboard reduces the distance between keys. These can be used in one hand or with two hands.	
Compact keyboard e.g. 'Cherry Keyboard'	Small keyboard for pupils that may just use one hand for typing or find it difficult to reach all the keys on a standard keyboard.	
Keyguard	e.g. available to fit standard keyboards, 'Cherry' keyboards and 'Big Keys Keyboards' Keyguards fit over a keyboard to prevent the user from accidentally striking keys. Also useful for pupils who have difficulty lifting their arms as they can drag their hand over the keyguard to find the right key.	Inclusive Technology Ltd

Mice

It may be helpful to consider using a wireless mouse to reduce the wires that may distract some pupils.

Changing the accessibility options of a mouse in the computer's operating system can give multiple options, e.g. changing the cursor size/format, slowing down the double-click speed. For further guidance talk to the school's ICT Technician or the LA Specialist Teaching Service for Physical Disability or see below.

Equipment	How could this help a pupil with cerebral palsy?	What might it look like?
Small size mouse, e.g. Education Mouse	A smaller mouse that suits little hands. Different coloured buttons assist with the understanding of left and right click.	Inclusive Technology Ltd

Joystick (These can be fitted with a joystick, T-bar or soft ball)	Designed for pupils with impaired motor skills. The joystick may be easier to grasp and can be configured for pupils who have difficulty with co-ordinating their movements and/or controlling the pressure used to action the joystick.	Inclusive Technology Ltd
Roller ball	The roller ball may assist students to control the cursor by providing a larger area to operate. A roller ball mouse can be fitted with a keyguard and made switch accessible.	Inclusive Technology Ltd
Hand-held track pads	This is another option for pupils with limited movement and pressure.	Inclusive Technology Ltd
Switches e.g. Jelly Bean Switches, Adjustable Tension Jelly Bean Switches, Suck/Blow Switches, Cushion Switches, Foot Switches	A switch can be positioned in different places according to the user's need, e.g. using an elbow to control the switch. If the pupil has a limited amount of pressure and/or movement these are really useful.	Inclusive Technology Ltd
Eyegaze system (This is a combined package of hardware and software.)	The pupil is able to control the cursor using the eye-operated software to communicate and record their work independently.	Inclusive Technology Ltd

It should be ensured that any ICT equipment is positioned correctly to enable the pupil to access it in the best way possible. The occupational therapist or the LA Specialist Teaching Service for Physical Disability will advise.

Software is the term used to describe programs or applications that can be used on a computer, laptop or tablet. There is a variety of ICT software available that may be beneficial. Some examples are described below:

Software	What does this software do?	What does this software look like?
Clicker 6 – available for laptops and as several iPad apps	Offers a multi-sensory approach of using words, pictures and sounds. Supports learning from letter level through to complex writing. (www.cricksoftware.co.uk)	 Inclusive Technology Ltd
Co Writer	Word prediction software that is compatible with MS Word and other applications. Contains a built-in text to speech reader, which can read letters, words and sentences.	
Penfriend	Penfriend is a screen reader with text magnification, word prediction and on-screen keyboards. Pupils can write faster as the software predicts the next word.	
Dragon Naturally Speaking	Speech recognition software that converts talk to text.	
Evernote	An app designed for note taking.	

Software to support skills development

Skill	What does this software do?
Keyboard skills e.g. BBC Dance Mat	A fun tool to develop touch typing skills.
Mouse skills e.g. 'Mouse Skills'	A game to support pupils who are developing their mouse control.

Changing the settings (as referred to above) in the 'Ease of Access Options', 'Keyboard' or 'Mouse' in the Settings panel may be sufficient to improve access.

Problems using the keyboard	Solution
The pupil has difficulty seeing the letters on the keys.	1. Raise the back of the keyboard, e.g. on a small angled board. 2. Purchase a set of yellow on black, or black on yellow stickers for the keys (upper or lowercase letters are available).
The pupil has difficulty activating two keys at the same time, e.g. using the shift key to get a capital letter.	*Sticky keys*
Pupil gets repeat letters/ deletions.	*Filter keys*
The pupil has difficulty seeing the cursor on screen.	*Settings – Devices – Mouse – additional options – mouse properties – pointer options*
The cursor moves too quickly for them to control it.	*Settings – Devices – Mouse – additional options – mouse properties – pointer options* *Control Panel – Ease of Access – Ease of Access Centre – Use the computer without a mouse or keyboard*
The pupil finds it difficult to open programs using 'double click'.	1. Slow down the 'double click' speed. *Settings – Devices – Mouse – additional options – mouse properties – buttons* 2. Select the icon with a single click on the mouse and then press the 'Return' key.
The pupil finds it difficult to select menu/window options using the mouse.	Teach keyboard shortcuts, e.g. use the 'tab' key to scan through the menus, the up/down arrow keys to scroll through the options and return to select.
The pupil is left handed or only has good use of the left hand.	Reverse the right and left button functions. *Settings – Devices – Mouse – additional options – mouse properties – buttons*

26 Developing fine motor skills

Many pupils with cerebral palsy will find it very difficult to develop efficient fine motor skills. The following activities should be encouraged in the early years setting and will need to continue for a longer period than most of their peers. It is acknowledged that some of the following activities will be problematic for some pupils, e.g. those with hemiplegia.

The following is a fine motor skill checklist with accompanying activities.

Skill area to be checked **Grasp** – can the pupil:	If not, try the following activities
• hold objects in a palmar grasp (whole hand) • use index finger in isolation (pointing)	– provide a wide range of toys to stimulate interest; encourage the child to reach out and grasp with both hands; – teach finger rhymes such as 'Two Little Dickie Birds'; – pick up and release a foam ball; – pick up and pass small ball from hand to hand; – use finger puppets on the index finger; – press keys of a toy telephone, till, toy musical instruments; – encourage finger painting; – encourage recorder playing/piano/keyboard playing; – teach keyboard/typing skills.
• hold objects in pincer grasp (index finger and thumb)	– pop bubble wrap between finger and thumb; – peg out washing (or paintings) to dry; – inset jigsaws (reducing in size); – bulldog clips to fasten paper; – sorting activities using small objects.
• hold a pencil in tripod grasp	– use activities above to develop a tripod grip; – try a range of pencil grips.

Other considerations • use finger and thumb in opposition • demonstrate acceptable finger/hand strength • rotate wrists/forearm **Hand dominance** – can the pupil: • demonstrate hand dominance	– touch each finger in turn using the thumb; – pick up small toys using tweezers or tongs; – roll plasticine or playdough between finger and thumb; – play with 'popper-beads'; – play with wind-up clockwork toys; – fasten press-studs on clothing. – squeeze playdough, stress balls; – playdough and plasticine activities; – tug of war; – water race where water is transferred from one container to another by filling and squeezing sponges; – hand jives/hand warm-up exercises; – squeezing citrus fruits on a traditional lemon squeezer; – chair press-ups; – write/draw with carbon paper underneath to encourage pressure; – offer squiggle pens and light pens, which give sensory feedback with sufficient pressure; – use of a paper punch and stapler. – nut and bolt toys; – wring out cloths and dolls' clothes; – look through a kaleidoscope; – sharpen pencils. – encourage two-handed scribbling; – observe pupil at play and present work from the side he/she favours more for using a phone, telescope and kicking a ball; – place a small white board end on to the pupil and get the pupil to draw patterns on both sides at the same time (after a week the stronger side will usually appear).
Mark making – can the pupil: *Remember children learn to imitate first then copy.* *Imitate = reproduce after a demonstration* *Copy = reproduce from model* • scribble to and fro holding pencil with palmar grasp • scribble and make dots holding pencil in pincer grasp • imitate vertical lines and sometimes V shapes	*Use a multi-sensory approach by selecting a range of activities taken from each of the sensory areas suggested below:* *Gross motor movement:* – play with cars and push-along toys; – wipe the table with damp cloth; swish hands in water and washing-up liquid to make bubbles;

	– make ribbon patterns in the air; – play marching games following the lines and direction of the desired pencil movement; – encourage visual tracking (following a moving object from left to right) with motorised remote control toys.
• imitate horizontal line	*Visual stimuli:* – demonstrate movements in the air asking the pupil to imitate your actions;
• imitate a circle	– demonstrate mark making on white boards then ask the pupil to imitate your marks; when this is achieved move on to copying.
• imitate 'T' and 'V' • draw horizontal and vertical lines	*Tactile (touch) stimuli:* – sand trays; – lentil, pasta trays; – playdough (see recipes); – finger paints (see recipes);
• copy 'O V H T' • imitate 'X' • copy 'X O V H T'	– shaving foam; – 'Roll 'n' Write' cards; – use template to colour within a shape; – use glue pens to form a raised outline for colouring within.
	Olfactory (smell) stimuli (check that the selected medium is child-friendly; exercise caution with essential oils): – use child-friendly scented crayons and markers;
• copy squares • copy triangles • write a few letters spontaneously	– use scented finger paints when providing tactile experiences; – experiment with fruit and vegetable printing to reinforce mark making and left to right tracking.
	Auditory (sound) stimuli: – use and reinforce directional language making sure the child understands when demonstrating up and down, forwards and backwards, over and under, left and right movements; – use 'listen and do'-type CDs that reinforce listening skills and fine motor skills.

Drawing skills – can the pupil:	Backward chaining/small-step approach
	Break the task into a series of small steps. For example, when teaching how to draw a face:
• draw a person with head and two more features	– provide a series of drawings of faces with one feature missing;
• draw a person with head, trunk, legs and usually arms and fingers	– ask the child to identify the missing feature; – demonstrate completion of the picture.
• draw a person with head, trunk, legs, arms, fingers and features	– ask the child to complete the picture; – gradually increase the complexity of the task by removing prompts.
• draw a house with windows, doors, roof and chimney	(The same model could be used for drawing a dog, cat, house.)
• draw a recognisable house	
• draw pictures with several items and show an indication of background	
• colour pictures staying mainly within the lines	
Bilateral integration (using two hands together sometimes, for different tasks) can the pupil:	
• hold an object in two hands and perform an action	– push a pram or a push-along toy; – hold steering wheel in toy car; – steer bike/trike by holding handle bars; – inset jigsaws.
• use one hand to steady an object while playing	– 'post' toys; – pretend and real baking (hold the bowl while stirring).
• hold an object in one hand while performing an action with the other	– peel a banana; – undo a zip; – sharpen a pencil; – use a hairdryer and hairbrush together; – hold a cup while pouring water into it from a jug.
• pour a drink from a bottle into a cup without spilling	– pour and fill a container with marbles, pebbles, conkers, lentils, sand, water play.
• remove and replace a screw-top lid	– nut and bolt construction toys; – café bar in home corner.

Crossing the midline This is an important element of bi-manual integration (using two hands together). This can be encouraged using the following activities.	– dressing up games; – dressing toys; – sit cross-legged and pat opposite knee; – march and touch opposite knee; – cut food with knife and fork; – activate activities; – sort activities where objects have to be picked up with one hand and placed in a container at the other side.
Hand-eye co-ordination – can the pupil: • build a tower with two cubes following a demonstration • build a tower of three cubes following a demonstration (sometimes spontaneously) • build a tower of six or seven cubes • build a tower of more than seven bricks using the dominant hand • build a bridge using three bricks after a demonstration • build towers of more than ten cubes • build bridges spontaneously using three bricks • build three steps using six cubes following a demonstration • thread a large needle • thread small beads	– provide play opportunities with building blocks, starting with large lightweight blocks; – provide a range of construction toys including self-adhesive varieties (Velcro/magnetic/interlocking); – gradually reduce the size of blocks/cubes; – use modelling and demonstration techniques to encourage creativity; – group pupils of differing abilities to provide positive role models. – provide a range of threading activities starting with dowel rods and progressing to stiffened cord and laces; – provide a range of bodkins and needles so that the pupil can select equipment within his/her skill level thus ensuring success and reinforcing self-esteem.

Developing handwriting

Handwriting may be difficult to develop but the following should be considered:

- Be aware of the order of skill development, i.e. the pupil should be able to produce certain shapes before handwriting is introduced.

Group 1

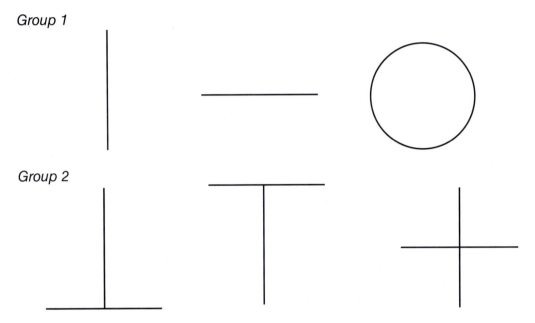

Group 2

- Develop the above patterns in a multi-sensory way:
  - pushing a car (left to right) across a 'race track';
  - make patterns with wet paintbrushes, playground chalks;
  - make patterns between tramlines of decreasing size with large felt tip pens, crayons;
  - use fingers in the sand to trace over writing patterns;
  - join dots on a whiteboard.
- Consider the use of the 'Write from the Start' programme to develop writing and perceptual skills (it may be necessary to enlarge the photocopied sheets).
- Use a structured handwriting scheme (printing will be easier than cursive script).
- Use 'apps' to develop letter formation. 'Letter School' utilises an errorless, multi-sensory approach.

Specialised fine motor equipment

Some (but not all) pupils with cerebral palsy who have difficulties in developing handwriting and manipulating standard classroom equipment, e.g. pencils, pens, scissors and rulers, may prefer to use specialist equipment to develop their skills and promote independence and confidence.

The standard tripod grasp is not always the most comfortable or achievable for some pupils. However, the pencil grasp *must* be relaxed and secure enough to allow the pupil to write

	A grasp should be changed only if it is tense, looks uncomfortable and causes pain after writing for ten or more minutes. Generally, children who wrap their thumbs or index fingers around the barrel of the pencil have an *insecure* grasp and would benefit from remediation. One alternative is to hold the pencil between index and middle fingers (the Monk's grip).

Make available a range of pencils with different-sized barrels (including maxi and triangular) for pupils to experiment with. A range of pens is also needed to try out – including gel ink pens as well as ballpoints, some with rubberised grips, since they each have a different 'feel' and what suits one pupil may not suit another.

	A selection of pencil grips should also be available – most schools have triangular grips available for use but often a moulded grip, which requires pupils to position their fingers correctly, is more beneficial.
	Sometimes the provision of an angled-board improves writing. To stop paper or books from sliding on the desk use either Blu-Tack or a rubberised non-slip mat.

Cutting skills

Pre-requisites

The child must be able to:

- open and close the hand;
- use both hands together (this will not always be possible for some pupils), with the dominant hand leading and the other hand assisting;
- isolate or combine the movements of thumb, index and middle fingers;
- co-ordinate arm, hand and eye movements;
- stabilise the wrist, elbow and shoulder joints to provide a base for hand movements;
- show evidence of imitating cutting movements in play situations.

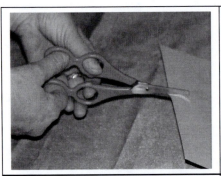	The most difficult action is to open the scissors again once the child has completed the cut. 'Trainer' scissors allow him/her to use both hands for cutting (see left) giving extra leverage. Alternatively, an adult may guide the child by placing his/her fingers in the first set of handle holes over the top of the child's hand.
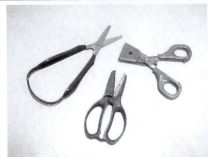	These scissors are all self-opening. From the left clockwise the picture shows the Peta looped scissors, Peta spring-loaded scissors and Fiskars nursery scissors. The pupil uses the whole hand to close the blades, giving maximum leverage. These increase confidence, especially if a pupil has low muscle tone and struggles to open and close standard scissors using two fingers only.
	With practice the pupil may progress to using scissors that have a larger, lower handle, thereby improving leverage. The scissors shown here are Fiskars Junior scissors and Hetty and Milly from the Berol range.
	Pupils with more severe physical difficulties may require 'table top' scissors. These are self-opening scissors, either mounted on a wooden or plastic block or resting on the lower horizontal bar. The only action required is to push down on the top horizontal bar.

27 Alternative recording strategies

Pupils with cerebral palsy may experience handwriting difficulties for a number of reasons: poor co-ordination, problems with visual perception, reduced muscle strength, increased tone, excessive fatigue and limited use of hand/upper limb resulting in poor letter formation and lack of fluency. They will have difficulty maintaining the pace of recording and coping with the volume of recording required. Most pupils will want to have a go at handwriting to be the same as their friends. It will quickly become obvious as to whether handwriting will be a viable method of recording in the long term. For some pupils with cerebral palsy handwriting will never be a viable alternative.

The following ideas can be used alongside conventional pencil/pen work or as complete alternatives:

- Help the younger pupil to type their name onto labels that they can independently place on their work.
- Use magnetic letters and numbers to create words and number sentences.
- Use word banks (with a limited number of words the pupil can read) to create short sentences and duplicate the words onto pieces of paper that the pupil can then stick into their workbook.
- Act as a scribe for the pupil as they dictate their work (it will be necessary to teach dictation skills).
- Share the recording of work (ICT or written) with a peer or an adult.
- Produce enlarged work sheets or handouts giving consideration to the colour and type of font and the colour of the paper the pupil finds the easiest to read from.
- Use a voice recorder to allow the pupil to tell a story or give information that can then be transcribed by the teaching assistant.
- Provide PowerPoint notes.
- Give pre-drawn diagrams that the pupil labels.
- Consider cloze procedure work, which requires the pupil to demonstrate knowledge by filling in blank spaces as necessary.
- Explore software such as the 'Clicker' program.
- Use ICT to record work, e.g. word processing or voice to text on a laptop, Netbook or iPad.
- Teach typing skills from an early age; try http://www.educatorstechnology. com/2011/07/best-free-educational-typing-apps-learn.html or BBC Dancemat (a free download).
- Explore the availability of apps for tablet computers (consult colleagues to share ideas). See http://www.inclusive.co.uk/apps.

- Investigate drawing/CAD packages to support D&T modules.
- A number of templates may be found in art shops or catalogues to support lettering or design production for D&T or Art, e.g. for GCSE course work.
- Consider voice recognition programs, e.g. 'Dragon Naturally Speaking'.

28 Teaching scribing skills

For many pupils, i.e. those with moderate to severe cerebral palsy, the most effective means of recording work is by dictation, especially with the increased demands at secondary level. However, dictating work, whether to a support assistant or using word recognition software, requires a level of skill, experience and discipline.

It is important that the support assistant does not anticipate the answer, extend or improve sentences, since the aim is to provide evidence of the pupil's level of attainment. Additionally, to get good grades in examinations pupils need to show the planning of an essay since this can add marks if there is not time to finish a question.

Pupils need to develop a series of skills in the following sequence:

Stage	To move to the next stage
The pupil dictates: • short phrases; • longer strings of phrases linked with 'and'; • grammatically correct short sentences; • longer grammatically correct sentences with one linking word, e.g. and, but, however, although; • sentences knowing when to indicate 'new sentence', 'full stop', 'comma', 'new paragraph'.	– discuss redrafting and ask the question who did what/when/where/why; – go over work and ask the pupil to break it up into shorter sentences based on the above; – use set/created Clicker grids to demonstrate links and sentence structure; – use 'story starts' and picture sequences to extend sentences; – read the pupil's work back and ask him/her to note breath pauses (full stop) and shorter pauses (comma), make it a game; – give the pupil a passage with no punctuation and ask him/her to punctuate.
Planning answers, the pupil: • can sequence a series of sentences describing an activity; • can identify the beginning, middle and end of a story; • can plan a short story by giving main points (written on 'Post-its') and organise these into an answer.	– use set/prepared Clicker grids; – give longer passages cut up and ask the pupil to sequence them; – use software e.g. 'Kidspiration', or 'Inspiration' for older pupils, to help the planning process.

29 Assessment

The assessment of some pupils with cerebral palsy can pose difficulties due to a number of issues. Difficulties with language skills can result in the pupil not understanding the task or being unable to respond in the required time. Restricted recording skills may make it difficult to respond to written questions in a conventional manner.

However, formative assessment is required in order to inform and facilitate learning by identifying personalised learning goals and to develop appropriate activities to meet these goals. Furthermore, assessment in some format will be considered necessary to show progress to parents, governors and bodies such as OFSTED.

Consideration should be given to how adjustments can be made to ensure the pupil demonstrates their knowledge and achieves the best results. For public or national exams, e.g. SATs and GCSEs, special access arrangements can be requested. Schools have to show that pupils need access arrangements, through assessment by a specialist teacher or an educational psychologist, to determine what support would be appropriate.

The following access arrangements can be requested:

- extra time and/or rest breaks;
- one-to-one or small group working;
- a quiet area;
- exam papers in different formats, e.g. digital format;
- support teachers to act as an amanuensis or reader.

If a laptop is the pupil's 'normal' way of working, its use in an examination situation does not need to be requested in advance.

Supporting the assessment process:

- give one-to-one work with a familiar support worker;
- provide concrete objects;
- use the normal method of recording, e.g. a laptop;
- provide a reader and a scribe;
- train support staff in the above.

The 'DFe 2014 Key stage 1 Assessment and Reporting Arrangements' state that any pupil below level 1 does not have to do the tests/tasks. A pupil above this but with SEN who cannot access the tests does not have to do them.

- Assessment and reporting arrangements Key Stage 2 (www.gov.uk) gives some guidelines for Key Stage 2 SAT testing.
- Teacher assessment should be used if standardised testing is not appropriate.

A range of assessment tools are available for tracking SEN pupil's progress:

Bsquared (www.bsquared.co.uk) is a standardised assessment package to help schools assess small steps of progress. It covers all areas of the curriculum.

PIVATs (www.lancashire.gov.uk) is a system to inform target setting for pupils of all ages whose performance is outside national expectations and can be used to complement work alongside statutory key stage assessment.

CASPA (www.caspaonline.co.uk) is a tool for analysis and evaluation of attainment and progress for pupils with SEN.

30 One page profiles

A One Page Profile is a summary of all the important information about a young person, captured on a single sheet of paper. Working with children with cerebral palsy to create a One Page Profile can help school staff to provide them with more person-centred care and support.

A One Page Profile usually has three headings: what people appreciate about me, what's important to me and how best to support me. Further information about One Page Profiles is available from Helen Sanderson Associates (www.helensandersonas-sociates.co.uk). Tools for supporting children to develop their own One Page Profile are available from this website.

In some settings staff are also encouraged to complete a One Page Profile. This can then be used to identify which staff may be best suited to supporting particular children. Having a One Page Profile can also help the people around you understand how best to support you at work and improve communication and relationships.

The following One Page Profiles illustrate the range of needs of pupils with cerebral palsy, from the mild to the more severe end of the continuum. Paul has an Individual Education Plan (IEP) to meet his needs. Louise does not have significant learning needs so does not require an IEP for learning issues. However, she does have a timetable that illustrates the support she needs to access the curriculum.

The following pages show One Page Profiles for Paul and Louise, Paul's IEP, examples of other formats for IEPs and a timetable to indicate the support required for Louise.

Paul

Age 5   Foundation Stage 2

What people appreciate about me	**What is important to me**	**How to support me**
Loving and affectionate Brilliant smile Chatterbox	Talking to my friends and the grown ups in my class. I might be difficult to understand sometimes but I like to tell my friends what I have been doing. • Fireman Sam and Peppa Pig are my favourite cartoon characters – when I'm tired it helps me to relax to watch these programmes for a little while. • My sister, Mummy, Daddy and my Nana are my family. I love going for a sleepover every other week at my Nana's house. She has a cat called Molly that I love. • I have just got a special trike that I love. It cost a lot of money but it is so much fun to ride. • I am not keen on messy things. I don't like gloop or foam or putting my hands in paint.	• I need a grown up to help me put on my foot supports each morning. • Because I am unsteady on my feet it helps me to have a grown up nearby to support me if necessary. • If I am walking a long way I need to use my wheelchair. • If I need to use my hands it helps me to sit down – otherwise I am working so hard to keep my balance that it makes doing writing or 'fiddly' tasks difficult. • I can use the toilet by myself but need a little bit of help to sort out my clothes. Making sure the floor isn't wet makes sure that I don't slip. • I am learning to write my name but need some practice of my letters. • I need help to do my exercises (Physical Management Plan) that my physiotherapist gives me. I need to do them every day. • When I'm cutting out I use special scissors (spring scissors). • Please let me eat my food by myself – but help me find my specially shaped spoon.

<table>
<tr><td>Louise

Age 10 in Year 6</td></tr>
</table>

What people like about me			
Confident	Outgoing and popular	Brave and determined	A friend to animals

What is important to me

- I go horse riding every week. My favourite horse to ride is called Ruby. She is a bit cheeky!
- I love my pets – I have two rabbits called Thumper and Lucky and a dog called Spot.
- My favourite band is One Direction – it is my dream to go and see them perform live. I would love to meet them.
- I like a lot of the same things as the other girls in my class, so it makes me happy when we hang out together and chat. I don't like being with a teaching assistant all the time.
- My Liberator communication aid is like part of my body – I cannot imagine being without it and when it goes wrong or breaks I get upset. Because I cannot talk with my mouth my machine is a necessity to me like a voice is a necessity to you.
- Getting to know me will help you understand me better. You will get to know my gestures and facial expressions and then we can get along well.

How to support me

- I have a powered wheelchair, a manual wheelchair and a walking frame. When I'm in my powered chair I am able to travel independently but need some help with opening doors and carrying equipment.
- I use a Stairclimber to get to my classroom on the second floor. The teaching assistants who work this machine need regular training to use it.
- For writing I need my laptop with keyguard and a specialist joystick. I use Clicker software to write as writing by hand is difficult for me. It helps me if the teacher has prepared in advance the materials I will need for my laptop.
- I need help with getting dressed and undressed and with eating and drinking.
- Training for me and my assistants on my communication aid is important. It needs to be charged regularly or the battery will run out.
- I can use some 'low tech' strategies to communicate, such as symbol boards that my speech and language therapist makes for me.
- I know when I need to use the toilet and can weight bear to move from my wheelchair to the toilet but I need enough space (the disabled toilet next to the cloakroom is best) and an assistant to help me with moving and adjusting my clothes.

31 Individual Education Plans

An Individual Education Plan (IEP) sets short-term targets for pupils whose needs are not met by ordinary provision within the classroom. The plan (sometimes also known as a 'Support Plan' or 'Pupil Passport') provides strategies and resources that school staff can use to support these pupils. Some pupils with cerebral palsy will require an IEP to meet their needs. The targets recorded should be SMART: Small, Measurable, Achievable, Realistic and with Timescales.

> The SEN and Disability Code of Practice 2014 states:
>
> Where it is decided to provide SEN support, and having formally notified the parents... the practitioner and the SENCo should agree, in consultation with the parent, the outcomes they are seeking, the interventions and support to be put in place, the expected impact on progress, development or behaviour, and a clear date for review. Plans should take into account the views of the child.

Schools have the flexibility to create their own IEP templates; there are some samples below. It is important that both pupils and parents are involved in the setting and reviewing of targets. This may be done on a termly basis, or more or less frequently depending on the needs of the pupil. Pupils should contribute to forming their targets and be aware of what they are. In some cases it may be appropriate to encourage pupils to carry out activities at home that support the targets.

Pupils with an Education, Health and Care Plan (EHCP) will have long and short-term outcomes that they are working towards. An IEP can be used to help pupil's achieve these outcomes by breaking them down into smaller steps. Following the Plan-Do-Review cycle (see figure below) may be helpful:

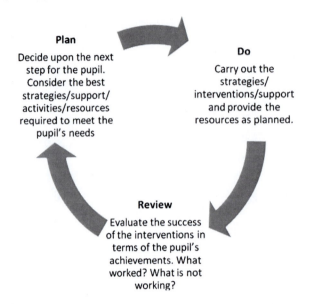

Plan
Decide upon the next step for the pupil. Consider the best strategies/support/activities/resources required to meet the pupil's needs

Do
Carry out the strategies/interventions/support and provide the resources as planned.

Review
Evaluate the success of the interventions in terms of the pupil's achievements. What worked? What is not working?

Other pupils will require a physical management programme, devised and monitored by a physiotherapist. This should maximise opportunities, e.g. a standing frame could be used when other pupils are standing in science lessons; exercises can be incorporated into warm-up activities in PE.

The following is an IEP for Paul, profiled above, a pupil in a mainstream school:

Primary School

Name: Paul

Date of Birth: 04.09.2011

Date: 12.12.2015

Review Date: 20.03.2016

Nature of the pupil's difficulties:

- Difficulty putting on lower garments after PE.
- Inability to form letters appropriately.
- Difficulty using scissors appropriately.

Targets	Strategies	Resources	Evaluation
I will be able to put on socks independently.	Teach through giving small step instructions, i.e. 1. Pull sock on over heel, Paul to pull sock up. 2. Put sock over instep, Paul to pull over heel. 3. Put sock onto toes, Paul to pull up. 4. Paul to put sock on with verbal prompts.	Practise with large sized socks	
I will be able to form a pattern of letters correctly (c, o, a, d)	Making large letter formations in the air. Overwriting letters in varied media. Copying/writing letters with various media, reduce letter sizes.	Foam, sand, finger paint. Chalk, felt tip pens, paint, triangular pencils.	
I will be able to cut along a wavy line	Cut between two slightly curved lines. Increase the bends in the lines. Decrease the gaps between the lines. Cut along a thick black wavy line.	Cutting sheets (card and paper) Specialist scissors (spring scissors)	

My Individual Education Plan

Things I find difficult	Things I like	My targets	How will you help me do this?	How did I get on?

This IEP format has been designed especially for the younger child. The idea is that the child's keyworker will spend some time discussing and writing the content in partnership with the child. This will help the child to feel more involved in their education and therefore increase motivation to achieve the targets that they have helped to set for themselves.

Child's name………………………………………..
Date of birth…………………………………………….
Date……………………………………………..
Review date………………………………………… IEP Agreed by:
Parent……………………………SENCo…………………………………………………

This would help a young child think of a target

INDIVIDUAL EDUCATION PLAN

Name ……………………………………

Date set ………………………….

Date to be reviewed ....

Child's strengths/can
dos………………………………………………………………………………………………………

………………………………………………

Child's targets	How to do it	Who will do it	How often	Resources needed	Outcome (to be completed for review meeting)
1.					
2.					

Date agreed:……………………………

Signed by parent/carers:…………………… Signed by SENCo: ……………………

IEP Review Notes:

Date of review: …………………………

Signed by parent/carers:…………………… Signed by SENCo: …………………

A timetable to show how additional adult support is used to facilitate Louise's access to the curriculum

	Registration	Numeracy strategy equipment required	Assembly	Break	Literacy hour equipment required	Lunch	Afternoon sessions equipment required	Break	Afternoon sessions equipment required
			Standing transfer to standard classroom				Louise free sitting during guided reading		Charge electrical equipment as necessary
Monday	SALT work	Use of Liberator Communication Aid throughout every day					**Technology** Access by Stairclimber Spring loaded scissors Non-slip mat		**History** Symbol board
Tuesday	Physiotherapy	Laptop with keyguard and joystick			Laptop with keyboard and joystick		**Geography** Laptop with keyboard and joystick Symbol board		**RE** Symbol board
Wednesday	SALT work	100 square grid					**PE** Physiotherapy in warm up Differentiated activities		**Science** Adapted equipment
Thursday	SALT work	X grid					**PE** Physiotherapy in warm up Differentiated activities		**ICT** PC laptop with keyguard
Friday	SALT work	(any other maths equipment as requested)					**Music** PC laptop		**ART** Spring loaded scissors Non-slip mat

Support staff assist with/supervise: • on-site mobility; • positioning and assisting with the manipulation of equipment; • oversight for break and lunchtime; • assist with personal hygiene routines; • implement physical management routines; • implement speech and language (SALT) routines.

Section 5

Support staff

32 Support staff: effective deployment

Not all pupils with cerebral palsy will require additional adult support in order to meet their needs within the classroom. However, for those pupils who have a more significant level of need, the provision of support staff is vital to ensure that their needs can be met.

> The Special Educational Needs and Disability Code of Practice, 2014 states:
>
> Where the interventions involve group or one-to-one teaching away from the main class or subject teacher they should **still retain responsibility for the pupil** working closely with any teaching assistants or specialist staff involved **to plan and assess the impact of interventions.**

Teachers may consider the following issues to ensure the most effective deployment of support staff:

- Support staff should promote independence at all times.
- It will not be necessary to work alongside the pupil in every lesson.
- Consider the position of support staff within the classroom: they may prompt the pupil or be in another part of the room to promote independent listening at whole class input.
- The pupil's focus should be on the teacher, rather than on support staff.
- Support staff should take notes during teacher input in order to reinforce key points at a later stage in the lesson.
- Support staff should monitor and record appropriate information about the pupil, e.g. physical performance, temperament.
- Liaison procedures between home and school should be established under the guidance of the SENCo/head of year/class teacher or form tutor.
- Support staff should work under the direction of the SENCo, class teacher or individual subject teachers.
- In practical sessions when the pupil needs to manipulate specialised equipment, support staff should work under the direction of the pupil.
- Withdrawal of the pupil for physical management routines should be negotiated with the SENCo and individual subject teachers.

The primary role of support staff is to facilitate independent learning and to enable the pupil to do as much as possible for him/herself. However, there are two further areas that contribute towards supporting a pupil with cerebral palsy.

Physical management

- assist with or supervise on-site mobility;
- set up equipment in the correct place;
- assist with transfers from one piece of equipment to another;
- implement exercise programmes overseen by the physiotherapist;
- monitor the seating position and ensure the correct positioning of equipment;
- assist with personal hygiene and cleansing routines (should be included in the job description);
- supervise in the playground;
- administer medication (should be included in the job description) and should follow the IHCP;
- check and store specialist equipment, e.g. slings;
- assist with feeding;
- operate equipment such as hoists and Stairclimbers;
- liaise with outside agencies, e.g. occupational therapist, physiotherapist, school nurse.

Training should always be given before any procedure, e.g. a physical manoeuvre or giving medication takes place. This should come from relevant professionals such as the physiotherapist, the LA Moving and Handling Specialist or the appropriate medical practitioner.

Classroom/curricular access

- support access to the curriculum through liaison with the class teacher;
- work on a one-to-one basis and in small groups;
- set up ICT equipment ensuring it is in the correct position for good access;
- ensure laptops are charged, work is printed;
- note key points;
- take notes/amanuensis;
- give verbal prompts;
- organise work sheets and resources to support the curriculum;
- support alternative recording strategies, e.g. photocopying PowerPoint notes;
- implement a speech and language programme;
- avoid creating dependency.

33 Support staff

Roles and responsibilities

Support staff should:

- **have a clear understanding of their roles and responsibilities**
  - have a knowledge of their job description;
  - work under the guidance of the teacher;
  - know that information given to parents should be with the knowledge of the class teacher;
  - respect the confidentiality of information about pupils;
  - maintain a professional demeanour with parents;
  - be aware of school policies with regard to behaviour, anti-bullying, Child Protection, etc.
- **be aware of the channels of communication within school**
  - ensure that information given by parents is relayed to SENCo/class teacher/ form tutor;
  - ensure that communication with outside agencies is carried out in consultation with the SENCo;
  - ensure that there is a mechanism for disseminating information to support staff about school activities, e.g. day book, staff room notice board, email.
- **be recognised as valued team members**
  - participate in the planning and monitoring process;
  - celebrate and share expertise.
- **be encouraged to make use of their personal skills**
  - share skills in the areas of ICT, organisation, creative arts.
- **be supported with appropriate on-going professional development opportunities**
  - observe and learn from other professionals;
  - take advantage of training opportunities in school and relevant external courses.
- **encourage the pupil's independence at all times:**
  - promote independent work habits;
  - promote independent life skills;
  - promote independent social skills.

34   Support staff: guidelines

Teaching staff and support staff should consider the following:

Avoid	but instead...
• sitting yourself next to the pupil in class at all times • offering too close an oversight during breaks and lunchtimes	• work with other pupils, whilst keeping an eye on the pupil you are assigned to • foster peer group relationships, e.g. a buddy system, introduce games including other pupils
• isolating the pupil by the positioning of any equipment • assuming that it is your responsibility to collect all equipment for the pupil	• ensure the pupil is part of the working group • where appropriate, encourage the pupil to organise and be responsible for their own work materials – peer group help is acceptable, have equipment easily available
• completing the task for the pupil	• ensure that the work is the pupil's, note the level of any adult input
• allowing inappropriate age behaviour, e.g. holding a pupil's hand in the playground and the school • making unnecessary allowances for the pupil • keeping a pupil in at break and lunchtimes – unless there is specific guidance	• give the minimum of physical assistance to ensure that the pupil is safe and can interact with peers • ensure that school rules apply to all • ensure that the pupil takes the opportunity to mix with friends, provide alternative activities with friends if indoor play is necessary
• making decisions for the pupil	• give the pupil the opportunity to make choices and decisions
• preventing the pupil from taking the consequences of their actions	• insist that the pupil takes the responsibility for and the consequences of their actions
• tolerating inappropriate behaviour such as bad language	• follow the school's behaviour policy, ensure the pupil is expressing unacceptable behaviour due to other reasons, e.g. frustration at not joining in games etc

Consider:

- who will determine what equipment is required and who will provide it;
- the training needed for staff to support the use of this equipment and who will provide the necessary training, e.g. specialist service for physical disability provide training for using Stairclimbers, hoists, moving and handling;
- the procedures for reporting any repairs and who is responsible for carrying out repairs, e.g. school site manager, wheelchair services, specialist teaching service for pupils with physical disabilities;
- who will determine when it is to be used;
- additional equipment may require appropriate storage, charging facilities.

Section 6

Independence skills

35 Feeding

Children with cerebral palsy may have difficulties with eating, swallowing, chewing and sucking. The speech and language therapist will give advice if the child has difficulties. Issues with balance and eye-hand co-ordination also make meal times more difficult. Access to the dining hall together with making choices and carrying trays may require assessment. The level of support required for mealtimes will depend on the needs of the individual pupil but independence to some degree should be encouraged whatever the level of ability.

Develop skills in the following ways:

- practise spooning sand, shaving foam, using appropriate sized and shaped spoons;
- slice soft food such as bananas before moving onto foods that give more resistance, e.g. apples;
- carry out two-handed activities (where possible), e.g. peeling a banana, pouring from a jug whilst holding a cup;
- roll playdough, plasticene and cut into sausage shapes with a knife and fork (again use appropriate cutlery; see below).

Developing strategies to make lunchtime easier to manage

- Ensure the pupil is seated appropriately; there must be support for balance and chairs must be at an appropriate height (elbows should be able to rest on the table). A bench may not be suitable and could make eating difficult and potentially dangerous. Some pupils will require specialist seating and the occupational therapist will advise.
- Packed lunches may be easier to eat but if a cooked lunch is preferred parents should have access to the weekly menu in order to rehearse choice making.
- Use appropriate cutlery, e.g. short moulded handles (IKEA cutlery), specialist adapted cutlery or put tubular foam onto handles to make them easier to grip or a 'spork', which combines a knife and fork (can be found in outdoor shops) together, for pupils who have restricted use of one hand.
- Specialist bowls and plates are available that are also easier for pupils with a weaker hand, e.g. a plate guard or a 'Manoy' dish.
- Use non-slip matting, e.g. Dycem™ or damp tea towel, to stabilise bowls and plates. Advice regarding equipment can be sought from the LA specialist teacher for physical disability service or the occupational therapist.

- It may be easier for pupils with limited mobility or wheelchair users to go to the dining hall first when it is quietest (with their friend). They may require help to make a choice of food, carry their tray (this could be done by an adult or peer) and find a place to sit.
- Ensure that this is a social occasion with peers rather than just sitting with the teaching assistant.
- Some pupils will be slow to eat their meals and miss out on playtimes, it may be possible to spread food intake out, e.g. have some at morning break, which would also help maintain stamina levels. It is essential that an appropriate level of food is consumed as many pupils with cerebral palsy expend a lot of energy.
- Some pupils may require feeding and they should decide whether they want to eat in a quieter area or in the dining hall.
- Have a paper towel or wipe available to clean hands and face at the end of a meal.

36 Dressing skills

Dressing for some children with cerebral palsy can be very problematic, depending on the range of muscles affected and difficulties with balance and visual perception. Some children will have support from an occupational therapist to develop skills. It is important to encourage a pupil to become as independent as possible, even if it is only putting on a hat or taking off a scarf.

The following can be considered in order to develop independence when dressing for PE or the outdoors (the level of the pupil's abilities will determine which are suitable).

- Develop movements for putting on clothes, e.g. quoits over wrists, ankles and hoops up to the waist and over the head, before practising dressing skills.
- Play games to practise skills, e.g. dressing up with large clothes in the house corner, starting with taking off hats.
- Practise doing fasteners on dolls that have large buttons, zips and Velcro fastenings or on dressing tabards.
- Skills should be taught in a hierarchical order where possible: hat, shoes, socks, trousers/skirt, T-shirt, jumper (learning to take off an item before putting it on).
- Younger pupils may benefit from having all their belongings, bags, hats in a particular colour or with a certain logo, in order for them to be found more easily in the cloakroom.
- Ensure the pupil is seated appropriately, e.g. in a chair/with their back to a solid surface/on the floor to gain balance.
- For pupils with a weaker side put the weakest arm/leg in first.
- It is easier to take off clothes than put them on, so develop this skill first.
- Backward chaining would be a useful method to teach the putting on of items of clothing, e.g. putting on trousers:
  - help the pupil put trousers on up to knees; pupil pulls the trousers up independently;
  - help the pupil put trousers on up to ankles; pupil pulls trousers up independently;
  - help pupil put one leg in; pupil continues;
  - pupil is shown how to lay trousers out and put them on;
  - pupil sits and puts trousers on independently.
- Encourage parents to dress their child in shoes with Velcro fastenings, trousers/ skirts with elasticated waist, school ties on elastic, clothes that are not tight (it may be necessary for uniform to have modifications to accommodate this).

- Promote independence by providing visual cue cards or lists to show what order clothes are taken off/put, on, e.g.

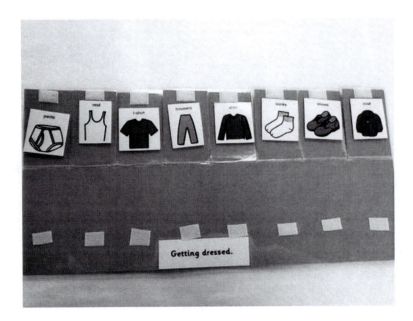

- Provide trays or baskets to put clothes in when changing for PE.
- Use T-shirts/sweatshirts with a logo/design on the front to help orientation of clothes.
- Give praise for effort when the pupil is trying to dress independently; only help the pupil when he/she has tried for him/herself.
- Teach the pupil how to ask for assistance.
- Ensure the pupil does not miss out on playtime, etc. if he/she is slow to dress.

Older pupils

- Older pupils need to develop coping strategies to overcome their difficulties.
- Clothes need to be considered carefully to enable the pupil to have credibility with his/her peers. Consider how fashions can be adapted to make dressing easier:
  - adapt clothes with elastic, Velcro, e.g. cut the school tie and join with Velcro;
  - adapt cuffs by putting in elastic to allow the hand to fit through;
  - use 'curly laces'.
- Some retailers supply school shirts with elasticated cuffs and top buttons.
- Schools may need to be flexible in their approach to uniform, as dressing for PE will be very difficult for some pupils, e.g. it may be possible for the pupil to wear track suit trousers on the day that PE takes place or at least not change after the lesson.
- Pupils who have difficulty with dressing and require support may prefer to use the physical management room for privacy and with equipment, e.g. grab bars for support.

37 Toileting

The degree to which children with cerebral palsy develop independent toileting will vary. Some will develop independent skills and others will not develop continence or will require high levels of support with specialist equipment to carry out toileting routines.

Some considerations can be made to develop independent skills

Advice should be sought from the occupational therapist, physiotherapist, specialist teaching service for physical disability, parents and the pupil.

Ambulant pupils

- It is essential that a child feels secure when sitting on the toilet; this can be achieved by using a toilet reducer and a footblock, which ensures that feet are on a flat surface. A more specialist footblock/toilet step may need to be wider than a commercially available one.
- Equipment that combines a reducer with steps and handles may be appropriate for some small children and is easily available (advice from professionals should be taken to ensure the suitability of such equipment).
- Grab bars fitted at the level the pupil can reach easily, when seated on the toilet, aid security.
- Lever taps are often easier to use.
- Some older pupils may prefer to use the accessible toilet; it should be ensured that they have easy access to the key if it is kept locked.
- Drop down bars (with a toilet roll holder attached) in the accessible toilet allow for independence.

Wheelchair users

Some wheelchair users may be able to develop independent transfers to the toilet using equipment such as a transfer board. Training will take place with the appropriate professional.

Those with more significant needs will require specialist equipment to transfer to the toilet; this may involve transfers from the wheelchair using a hoist and sling, illustrated below.

Training from a specialist, e.g. the LA moving and handling specialist in the use of this equipment is essential.

Guidelines for staff providing intimate personal care for children and young people

Duty of Care

The Children's Act 2004 places a duty on organisations to safeguard and promote the welfare of children and young people. This includes the need to ensure that all adults who work with or on behalf of children and young people in these organisations are competent, confident and safe to do so.

Safeguarding Children and Safer Recruitment in Education, 2010 also encompasses issues such as pupil health and safety and bullying, about which there are specific statutory requirements and a range of other issues, e.g. arrangements for meeting the medical needs of children with medical conditions.

Intimate personal care

Intimate personal care includes hands-on physical care in personal hygiene, and physical presence or observation to support procedures during such activities. Some pupils may require support with personal care on either a short, longer term or permanent basis due to SEN and disability, medical needs or a temporary impairment. This could include:

- pupils with limbs in plaster;
- wheelchair users;
- those with pervasive medical conditions.

Intimate personal care tasks can include:

- 'body bathing' other than to arms, face and legs below the knee;
- toileting, wiping and care in the genital and anal areas;
- dressing and undressing;
- application of medical treatment, other than to arms, face and legs below the knee;
- supporting with the changing of sanitary protection.

Guidance when supporting children and young people who require reasonable adjustments to be made in arrangements for personal care can be found under the relevant legislation, e.g. Early Years, Foundation Stage (2012), Equality Act (2010) and Supporting pupils with a medical condition in school, 2014.

The medical needs of the pupil will be defined in the Individual Health Care Plan and a specific **Intimate Care Plan** will be required to determine the exact requirements.

The following considerations should be made:

- the dignity of the pupil is maintained at all times;
- procedures are sensitive to their needs and preferences and their views are taken into consideration, e.g. their preference for a male or female support worker;
- the pupil should be able to give consent or withdraw from procedures;
- safety and comfort should be ensured during the procedure, e.g. the pupil should be on a safe changing place and access it with correct moving and handling procedures;
- safeguarding procedures should be followed in order to protect the pupil from abuse;
- also, staff should be protected from allegations; ideally two members of staff should be present;
- the pupil should be encouraged to care for themselves as much as they are able;
- the diversity of individuals and communities should be valued and respected and no discrimination should take place.

Facilities and resources

There must be suitable hygienic changing facilities for changing any children, the necessary resources should be included in a school's/ setting's Access Plan.

Disposing of nappies/pads

Guidance from the Health and Safety Executive, 'Managing Offensive/Hygiene Waste' (January 2009), is that any disposal of waste for one child can be in the usual bins using appropriate nappy sacks. The waste would be considered to be municipal waste. For wet nappies a single bag is sufficient but soiled nappies require double bagging. Any more than this and schools will need to make special arrangements.

Agreeing a procedure for personal care in school

Intimate care in schools can be provided only by those who have specifically (either as part of their agreed job description or otherwise) indicated a willingness to do so. No employee can be required to provide intimate care.

Schools should have clear, written guidelines for staff to follow when changing a child so that staff are not put at any unnecessary risk.

Written guidelines should detail:

- who will carry out intimate care procedures (to include more than one person to cover for absence);
- where care will take place;
- resources that will be required and who will provide them;
- how nappies/pads etc. will be disposed of;
- how other wet or soiled clothes will be dealt with;
- infection control measures that are to be put in place;
- safeguarding procedures, e.g. what a member of staff will do if the child is unduly distressed or if marks or injuries are noticed;
- written agreements with parents about intimate care procedures;
- appropriate training for certain procedures, including catheterisation, which should come from health care staff and details included in the Individual Health Care Plan.

Staff should take care (both verbally and in terms of their body language) to ensure that the pupil is never made to feel insecure.

Intimate care arrangements should be discussed with parents/carers on a regular basis and recorded on the child's Intimate Care Plan. The needs and wishes of children and parents will be taken into account, wherever possible, within the constraints of staffing and equal opportunities.

The setting/school should ensure that sufficient disposable resources are available, for example:

- antiseptic hand cleanser;
- paper towels;
- disposable aprons and gloves;
- nappy bags/sacks;
- cleansing equipment for infection control;
- disposal bin.

Parents/carers will provide:

- medical supplies as required;
- a supply of spare nappies/pads and wipes;
- spare clothes.

Intimate Care Plan

A pro forma can be found in the Appendix.

Off-site visits

Checks should be made beforehand to ensure that there are suitable facilities for intimate care available on any off-site visit, short or extended (also see chapter Off-site activities).

It will also be necessary to consider how intimate care can be dealt with in relation to PE, swimming, after school clubs, transport to and from school etc.

Confidentiality

Parents and staff should be aware that matters concerning intimate care will be dealt with confidentially and sensitively and that the young person's right to privacy and dignity is maintained at all times.

For more detail see **'Guidelines for staff providing intimate care for children and young people, 2013 gov.uk'.**

38 Physical management room

Some pupils with cerebral palsy will require access to a physical management room to meet their intimate care needs. The local authority specialist teaching service for physical disability should be consulted with regard to fitting out and organisation of the physical management room. The following should be taken into consideration.

- The doorways should be wide enough for a wheelchair to pass through easily.
- The size of the room is important and so is accessibility – a wheelchair user/child with a walking aid should be able to get in and turn around.
- There should be enough space for two carers when supporting a pupil with using the toilet. Schools should be aware that architects planning new buildings work to comply with the minimum standards set out in the Disability Discrimination Act (DDA 1995); this minimum standard is not suitable for school support rooms. For instance, toilets should be positioned so that carers can access them from either side, rather than being placed in the corner.
- The toilet needs to be at the correct height for access with suitable handrails fitted.
- The toilet area may have to accommodate pupils with a variety of different needs – pupils with incontinence problems, catheter users, pupils who need moving from wheelchair to toilet using a hoist and sling.
- A manual hoist or ceiling tracking hoists that enable a pupil to be transferred from one area to another, e.g. from wheelchair to toilet without an adult lifting the pupil.
- There should be room for a changing table/hydraulic plinth with sides. This may be needed in conjunction with a ceiling track hoist, when dressing or undressing a pupil, or for physiotherapy exercises to take place. The plinth needs to be centrally situated to allow access from both sides and away from hazards. For example, it would not be appropriate to position a plinth next to a radiator.
- The child should be able to access the sink and taps independently.
- The child should be able to dry their hands (using either paper towels or a drier) and use the mirror independently.
- There should be enough room to allow supervision with privacy. For example, there could be a screened off area within the toilet (a shower curtain would suffice) to allow adults to remain in the room but give the pupil some privacy.
- Suitable heat, light, ventilation should be within the room.
- The support assistant should be able to call for help if required by use of an emergency alarm system.

- A cupboard should be available to store items in, e.g. aprons, gloves, nappies, catheters etc. A suitable disposal bin for soiled or clinical waste will be required.
- A physical management room is not for the sole usage of one pupil so equipment should be cleaned after usage and waste disposed of appropriately.

The equipment used within the room will need to be adequately serviced and maintained. Refer to the following link with regard to safety and maintenance: http://www.hse.gov.uk/work-equipment-machinery/loler.htm

Prior to any staff using a support room, they need to be adequately trained in moving and handling skills and also how to use the equipment within the support room. Liaison between the school, Local Authority, Specialist teaching service for physical disability and the NHS Therapy Services will be required in order to develop manual handling plans for staff to follow in order to maintain theirs and the pupil's safety during transfers.

Section 7

Pupils and parents

39 Developing self esteem

The Oxford Dictionary's definition of self esteem is... 'Confidence in one's own worth or abilities.'

'A child's ability to form good relationships not only enhances their personal development but helps them progress intellectually... Equipping children to understand and articulate their own identity, take the perspectives of others, and recognise their rights and responsibilities in the social worlds they inhabit, we are preparing them to cope confidently with their own future lives and to contribute to the future of their communities.' (Burrell and Riley 2005)

Pupils who have an appearance that is physically different may have (or be at risk of) having difficulties forming relationships or be victims of bullying. As a result of this they may not feel confident about themselves or how they look, which in turn may lead to low self esteem and unhappiness. The adults who work with pupils with cerebral palsy are in a prime position to monitor and affect the self esteem of these children. They are able to inform and challenge the views of others to ensure that a positive environment is available for pupils with cerebral palsy to thrive, develop and feel a valued member of the community.

High or low levels of self esteem can affect how an individual faces new challenges and influence their feelings as a learner, towards school, their peers and their future.

The following strategies may help to build self esteem:

- Ensure all staff are aware of the pupils' needs/abilities/limitations. It is important to understand that they are not being lazy, they are not ignoring the adult and they most certainly are not being naughty. Understanding the pupil will help form the attitude of the adults who work with them, which in turn will foster good relationships. A One Page Profile is an effective way of doing this.
- Every child is unique; working with a pupil with cerebral palsy in the past does not mean they are the same as the child in the class now. They have cerebral palsy but that may be where the similarities end.
- Does the pupil understand what cerebral palsy is? An understanding of the condition and acceptance of the disability is linked to increased self esteem. Discuss with parents and other professionals how much the pupil understands and how they can be supported to see the positive aspects of cerebral palsy.

- If opinions are asked for then listen to the pupil; act on it. Don't nod and agree; value what is said and try to implement what has been suggested. If this is not possible then explain why not, don't just take no notice of it.

- Make time to listen. It may take a pupil with cerebral palsy longer to explain what they mean. They may forget the words or put them in the wrong order. They may appear as if they have gone off track but it is important to take the time to focus on what is being said; it may be a conversation ago and the processing time is making it appear as if the pupil is not listening. Recap the conversation, offer prompts to encourage responses.

- Discuss goals with the pupil. Encourage them to set their own goals. Make them attainable but they need to be challenged as does any child.

- Set work at an appropriate level; if they are working below the age-related expectations then targets should be where they are working at not at the chronological age.

- Try to make worksheets look age appropriate or as close in appearance to the other pupils' work as possible.

- Know the pupil. Observe any difficulties they may have, assess, rethink, differentiate and repeat the activity if necessary.

- Recognise progress may be slow and reached by small steps. Acknowledge and celebrate success whenever it is achieved; this could be personally, with parents or on a wider school community level.

- Celebrate good work and display it. Work can be shared in many different ways: writing, using ICT, audio recordings and video. Think out of the box when looking for ways to share work.

- Offer peer mentoring training. Make the pupil the expert in their own area; someone who can share this knowledge with their peers.

- Consider vulnerable times, e.g. when other children may be running around at play times, and if necessary offer alternative activities or a buddy system so that the pupil is not alone.

- Establish the pupil's strength and build on it. It may be using ICT; they could lead sessions on 'how to....'

- Consider times when the pupil may feel different or left out, e.g. PE lessons, sports days. Be inventive – think of differentiated activities that everyone will enjoy, rather than just making them the photographer or using the time for the physiotherapy exercises. There will be some inclusive sports locally; find out what is available from your Local Authority Specialist Teaching Service for Disability.

- Optimise the learning environment. Consider access to equipment, mobility around the room and independent working when possible. A pupil with cerebral palsy will not want or need an adult beside them at all times. Ask 'How can I help?' don't just jump in and do.

- Encourage independence skills; they may need short programmes to develop self help skills or personal care skills but by working on these areas the pupil will feel more confident.

- If personal care is required, i.e. toileting, changing or feeding, then is it appropriate to have a female support? Ask the pupil what they want; most teenage boys would prefer a male 1:1 assistant for this type of support (and vice-versa).

- Consider creating an information book about the pupil (it is essential to discuss this with parents and the pupil). The child is the expert on him or herself; they often feel very proud after creating an information book about themselves to share with the staff and their friends. This is their opportunity to express what they find challenging and why and how they can be helped to overcome this.

- Involve the pupil in any changes that may take place, particularly at times of transition. This time in their lives can be scary and may be quite daunting. Ensure that they are fully involved in decisions and make an early start to the transition.
- The school or Local Authority Specialist Teaching Service for Disability may provide a course that raises self-esteem.
- Teenagers with cerebral palsy sometimes become isolated as their peers can easily access parties etc. Try to ensure the pupil joins in after-school activities and all school visits.

40 Emotional issues

There is some overlap in self-esteem and emotional issues; it may be necessary to consider the two together.

Issues that may arise:

- frustration at not being able to participate in activities in the same way as their peers;
- the time it takes to do everyday tasks such as going to the toilet;
- resentment as there is growing awareness of the restrictions their disability brings;
- difficulty establishing friendships and making relationships with the opposite sex as they get older;
- having to rely on adults for hygiene routines, dressing etc. rather than being independent;
- the onset of puberty with all its ramifications;
- low self-esteem.

Strategies and practical help

- See the section on self-esteem.
- Let the pupil know it is all right to feel frustration etc.
- Help them to understand the changes that are happening and why.
- Give the pupil the vocabulary to explain how they are feeling. Identify and discuss emotions; explore them and consider appropriate ways of dealing with them. Help to understand what they are and how we can control them.
- Discuss what makes the pupil feel good and celebrate it.
- Encourage a support buddy – an allocated adult who will listen. Ensure the pupil knows this person and is comfortable talking to them.
- Ensure the relevant teaching staff are aware of any issues raised and enlist their help.
- Discuss relevant issues (with the pupil's agreement in circle time or PSHE lessons).
- Discuss possible strategies to overcome or at least lessen some of the frustrations.
- Liaise with parents to try to find possible solutions.

41   Promoting peer group relationships

There may be some factors that inhibit some pupils with cerebral palsy from fully integrating with their peers:

- restricted mobility, which prevents them joining in playground games;
- use of a wheelchair;
- adult oversight to ensure safety but which inhibits peer interaction;
- limited receptive and language skills.

It may be necessary to consider ways to encourage good relationships between peers, through a variety of methods.

- Ensure adults value the pupil and their contributions and thereby set a good example.
- In Foundation Stage and Key Stage 1, develop other pupils' awareness of their peer with cerebral palsy, by sharing a personal book compiled by the parents or with their support, during circle time. Published books must be discussed first with parents and used with great sensitivity.
- If there are any issues with social interaction in Key Stage 2, set up a friendship group of pupils who would like to play with the pupil with cerebral palsy. Weekly meetings could be held to discuss any positive features or difficulties. It may be necessary to support the group the pupil is choosing to play with.
- Be aware that speech and language difficulties and physical limitations, limited hand function, can be a barrier to developing relationships and that it may be necessary to encourage play with other pupils with guidance of how to play.
- Have a 'buddy' to help open doors, collect equipment.
- Have useful jobs that pupils and their peers can share.
- Provide equipment that is accessible to all pupils, e.g. larger, soft ball if they want to play catch or a very large ball if they want to play football from their wheelchair. Table top games will also be appropriate.
- Have a coned area to protect those whose unsteady gait makes them vulnerable. Adults should be sensitive to the pupils need to have 'space' at break times.
- However, if the pupil does appear to be isolated, organise structured play sessions led by a support assistant in the playground, e.g. boccia.
- Provide alternative options at playtime if pupils cannot be outside in inclement weather (those with restricted mobility may find it difficult to be safe or keep warm). Ensure that there are friends to play with.

- Encourage co-operative learning by working with a partner or in a small group. Share out the tasks, e.g. the pupil with cerebral palsy contributes verbally but shares the recording of the ideas with others in the group.
- Use peer support instead of adult support whenever possible.
- Encourage participation in lunchtime or after-school clubs.
- Encourage self-awareness, identity, self-esteem and self-confidence.

42 The emotional aspects of life with a child with cerebral palsy

It can sometimes be several months after birth that a child is diagnosed with cerebral palsy. Families respond to the diagnosis of cerebral palsy in their own individual ways. In the months and years that follow, the families start the process of readjustment. Many of the emotions experienced will follow a pattern similar to that of bereavement and each family member may be at a different stage in the process of understanding and accepting the needs of their child.

- Initial feelings of grief are usually for the child that they thought they would have and now have lost.
- Acceptance of their child and coming to terms with his/her difficulties follows the realisation that children with cerebral palsy are first and foremost children but that they need more help to overcome their problems.
- Grief may resurface at different milestones in their child's life, e.g. at secondary transition.
- Caring for a child with cerebral palsy with more significant difficulties can be very tiring, e.g. there are moving and handling issues that become more difficult as the child becomes heavier.
- There may be physical management programme to follow, e.g. exercises and the use of specialist equipment. The child may be resistant to this at home.
- Outings and holidays can be very difficult, e.g. bulky equipment may need to be taken, lifting a child in and out of a car gets harder, accessing an aeroplane needs extra planning.
- Parents attend very many appointments with their children and this can be emotionally exhausting as each is a reminder of a layer of difficulty faced by them and their child.
- Parents often get very weary of being more expert than the experts and having to fight to access appropriate levels of care for their child.
- Accessing child care and/or baby sitters may be more difficult than for other parents.
- Extended family members may question the approaches suggested by professionals, intended to support the child and its family, thus undermining the parents, and leaving them feeling isolated.
- As the parents look to the long-term future there will be anxiety about what will become of their child.

43 Siblings of the pupil with cerebral palsy

Children who have a brother or sister with cerebral palsy may need special consideration in school.

- Changes in their behaviour may indicate they are experiencing emotional difficulties that are related to issues around their sibling with cerebral palsy, and they may require understanding and support.
- They may feel that things are not fair and more attention is given to their sibling with cerebral palsy.
- They may feel embarrassed about their brother or sister, on some occasions.
- They may take undue responsibility for their sibling.
- They may worry about their brother or sister.
- They may feel unduly protective towards their brother/sister and demonstrate anger at pupils who try to tease or bully (any issues should be addressed at school).
- Some children may feel guilty about their feelings for their brother/sister.
- They may be teased or bullied because of a sibling with cerebral palsy (any issues should be addressed at school).

44 Home/school liaison

> Early years providers, schools and colleges should fully engage parents and/or young people with SEN when drawing up policies that affect them. Enabling parents to share their knowledge about their child and engage in positive discussion helps to give them confidence that their views and contributions are valued and will be acted upon.
>
> (Special Educational Needs and Disability Code of Practice, 2014)

There are a number of considerations that can be made in order to foster good home/school partnerships.

- Value the information that parents give about their child.
- Parents should be aware of the Special Educational Needs and Disability Code of Practice, 2014 and its implications for them.
- They should be invited to contribute to Learning Support Plans/IEP, attend review meetings and discuss how they can support the LSP/IEP.
- Ask for contributions and provide reports for parents prior to reviews of EHC plans.
- Parents should know whom to contact if they have concerns about their child, for example:
    - class teacher;
    - SENCo;
    - head teacher;
    - special needs governor.
- Parental concerns should be listened to, acknowledged and addressed.
- Issues, initiated by either school or parents, should be raised at an early stage so that an early resolution can be made.
- Involve parents if the pupil is perceived to be having difficulties in school and seek co-operative solutions.
- Inform parents of visits from other professionals, e.g. educational psychologist, speech and language therapist, and ensure any relevant reports are shared.
- Consult parents when changes in provision are being considered.
- Plan transition to new classes, new schools together.
- Ensure parents are aware that their child's work is valued, e.g. through including his/her work in displays.
- Use a home/school diary (either a paper or electronic format) to allow school and home to create a dialogue about the pupil's home and school life, particularly if there are restricted language skills. This should preferably be written in the

first person (for the younger pupil) so the child is sharing the story of their day, e.g. "I painted a picture, I spoke in assembly." For older pupils comments may be in the school journal or it may be more appropriate to have a separate diary for more personal comments other than homework requirements.

- Avoid discussions about their child within the hearing of other parents. Pupils should not hear any negative comments about themselves.
- Give positive messages to the parent about their child. If problems arise, find solutions in a productive manner.

Section 8

Transition to adulthood

45　Transition to adulthood

> Pupils should be supported … in decisions about their transition to adult life. They should also be involved in discussions about the schools and colleges they would like to attend. EHC plans should reflect this important ambition.
> (Special Educational Needs and Disability Code of Practice, 2014)

Local authorities, education providers and their partners should work together to help children and young people achieve successful long-term outcomes, such as getting a job or going into higher education, being able to make choices about their support and where they live, and making friends and participating in society. Raising aspirations is crucial if young people are to achieve these goals.

It is important that the following considerations are made to allow the correct provision to be made for the young person's future.

- Planning needs to start early on, from Year 9 in school at the latest. Pupils with an EHCP (and those without) should have a review during which planning for the future is discussed.

The following should be considered:

  - current skills and interests;
  - future education;
  - employment;
  - housing.

- Some pupils may lack the cognitive ability to make decisions about their future and will need the support of parents or an advocate to do so.
- The accessible method of communication for the pupil should be taken into consideration.
- Pupils may have difficulty considering the possibilities for their future and dealing with change; role models with the same interests may provide ideas.
- Providing experiences may make possibilities more real, e.g. work experience, further education placements, types of accommodation.
- The Children and Families Bill gives significant rights directly to young people once they reach 16. When a young person is over 16, local authorities and other agencies should normally engage directly with the young person, ensuring that as part of the planning process, they identify the relevant people who should be involved, and how to involve them.

For those moving to further education the Special Educational Needs and Disability Code of Practice, 2014 suggests:

- the involvement of staff from the college's learning support team in the school-based transition reviews;
- an orientation period during the summer holidays, to enable the student to find his way around the college campus and meet the learning support staff;
- opportunities to practise travelling to and from college;
- the development of an Individual Learning Programme outlining longer-term goals covering all aspects of learning and development, with shorter-term targets to meet the goals;
- supported access to taster sessions over a first year in college;
- a more detailed assessment of the young person's needs and wishes provided by learning support tutors during a 'taster' year;
- staff development to ensure an understanding of the student's particular method of communication;
- use of expertise in access technology to identify appropriate switches, communication boards to facilitate the student's involvement in an entry level course;
- courses normally covered in one year planned over two years to meet the young person's learning needs.

When a young person with an EHC plan takes up a place in higher education, their Education Health and Care Plan will cease. Local authorities should plan a smooth transition to the higher education institution concerned (and, where applicable, to the new local authority area) before ceasing to maintain the young person's plan. Once the young person's place has been confirmed at the higher education institution, the local authority **must** (with the young person's permission) pass a copy of their EHC plan to the relevant member of staff.

46 Work opportunities

An effective way to prepare young people with SEN for employment is to arrange work-based learning that enables them to have first-hand experience of work.

The following could be considered:

- Apprenticeships: Young people with EHC plans can retain their plan when on an apprenticeship.
- Traineeships: education and training programmes with work experience, focused on giving young people the skills and experience they need to help them compete for an apprenticeship or other jobs. Traineeships last a maximum of six months and include core components of work preparation training, English and maths (unless GCSE A*–C standard has already been achieved) and a high-quality work experience placement. They are open to young people aged 16 to 24, including those with EHC plans.
- Supported internships: structured study programmes for young people with an EHC plan, based primarily with an employer. Normally lasting for a year and include extended unpaid work placements of at least six months. Wherever possible, they support the young person to move into paid employment at the end of the programme. Students complete a personalised study programme that includes the chance to study for relevant substantial qualifications, if suitable, and English and maths to an appropriate level. Those with EHC plans will be able to retain their plan when undertaking a supported internship.

When considering a work placement as part of a study programme, such as a supported internship, schools or colleges should match students carefully with the available placements. A thorough understanding of the student's potential, abilities, interests and areas they want to develop should inform honest conversations with potential employers. This is more likely to result in a positive experience for the student and the employer.

Schools and colleges should consider funding from Access to Work, available from the Department for Work and Pensions, as a potential source of practical support for people with disabilities or health (including mental health) conditions on entering work and apprenticeships, as well as the in-work elements of traineeships or supported internships. More information is available from the gov.uk website and the Preparing for Adulthood website.

In preparing young people for employment, local authorities, schools and colleges should be aware of the different employment options for disabled adults. This should include 'job-carving' – tailoring a job so it is suitable for a particular worker and their skills.

Help to support young people with SEN into work is available from supported employment services who provide expert, individualised support to secure sustainable, paid work. This includes support in matching students to suitable work placements, searching for a suitable job and providing training (for example, from job coaches) in the workplace when a job has been secured.

Education and training should include help for students who need it to develop skills that will prepare them for work, such as communication and social skills, using assistive technology, and independent travel training. It can also include support for students who may want to be self-employed, such as setting up a micro-enterprise.

Where a young person may need support from adult services, local authorities should consider undertaking a transition assessment to aid discussions around pathways to employment.

Refer to the Special Educational Needs and Disability Code of Practice, 2014 for full guidance on establishing work placements.

Section 9

Continuing Professional Development

47 Planning for Continuing Professional Development (CPD)

As a pupil with cerebral palsy enters a school it is important that all staff (including teaching assistants, lunchtime supervisors and support staff) feel able to meet their needs. The provision of carefully tailored CPD will help to build colleagues' knowledge and enable the pupil to be appropriately supported.

An outline plan of CPD sessions might incorporate objectives such as ensuring that colleagues have:

- a sound knowledge of the definition and implications of cerebral palsy;
- the particular profile of the pupil;
- the confidence to ask experienced colleagues for help and advice;
- a range of strategies to meet individual needs and reduce barriers to learning.

Format of CPD

The method of delivering professional development will depend on particular factors relating to the school as a whole, and to individual teachers and teaching assistants. The opportunity to learn more about children with cerebral palsy will develop confidence within the staff. For pupils with more complex needs, training will be needed from a variety of professionals.

There are many different formats of CPD to consider:

- **Whole-staff training during a CPD day, or staff meeting**: This could be delivered by several professionals including the Local Authority Specialist Teaching Service for Physical Disability and therapists involved with the pupil. If this option is chosen, give details of previous training received by staff.
  A school's SENCo is often the best person to organise such training as he or she knows the school, the staff and the children, and can ensure that information and advice offered is relevant and appropriate. Such a person can also build in opportunities for follow-up and on-going development. Be 'in it together'; mutual vulnerability can be a powerful medium for exploring how changes to practice can result in positive developments.
- **A specifically identified group training:** These would be scheduled sessions for specific staff and would be focused on learning to use a specific approach or resource. It would be delivered by an expert in the field, e.g. the Specialist Teaching Service for Physical Disability's Moving and Handling Trainer who would train

relevant staff in moving and handling procedures and the correct use of equipment such as hoists and slings.

- **Sharing best practice** (sometimes referred to as 'joint practice development' – JPD): This is more about working together than about transferring knowledge or tips from one educator to another. Activities such as peer observation and shared planning can help to develop a sense of common purpose among staff.
- **Individual mentoring/coaching:** This can be particularly useful where a colleague is teaching a pupil with cerebral palsy and has no previous experience of this particular condition.
- **Individual study:** Colleagues who strive to make good provision for pupils with cerebral palsy can become very interested in finding out more, even developing expertise in the field. Pursuing a course of study at university, attending a specific course or locally provided training should be encouraged and supported – with the proviso that there will be some form of dissemination to colleagues. This course of action can be particularly beneficial to teaching assistants tasked with delivering intervention programmes and/or supporting individual children with CP.
- **Encourage professional reading** in small groups or individually. Place new relevant books (including this one!) in the staffroom library; seek out and share articles and research studies as food for thought, as well as reviews of useful resources. Perhaps devote five minutes of meeting time to highlight why you have selected particular reading matter. Encourage staff to contribute to this process too. Perhaps use social networking or your school's virtual learning environment to facilitate it.

An outline for whole-school training on cerebral palsy

Training may be sought from the professionals involved with the pupil. It could involve:

- an overview of the condition;
- a specific description of the pupil/s who will attend the school;
- input from the pupil themselves;
- the role of professionals involved;
- the adjustments that will need to be made to the environment and the curriculum;
- examples of specialist equipment required to allow access to the curriculum;
- the role of support staff.

Further work could include:

- asking colleagues if they have ever been in a situation where their mobility has been impaired or if they have been in a situation where it has been difficult to make themselves understood;
- giving an overview of the pupil's condition and asking staff to write down the difficulties they feel the pupil would encounter within their school, including getting to and from school;
- discussing classroom strategies: putting together a good practice guide;
- considering the effective use of teaching assistants;
- ensuring staff are familiar with what happens during any specialist sessions; can colleagues observe an intervention group in action? How can they support and reinforce this work?

- thinking of some ways to enhance the self esteem of the pupil with CP;
- gaining parents' support and help them to help their children.

Evaluating and following up CPD

Whichever mode of CPD is delivered (a mixed menu may be preferred), it's important to evaluate its effectiveness and plan for on-going development. Consider a short evaluation sheet for staff to complete after a training session on cerebral palsy, including their suggestions and requests for further development opportunities.

Taking this information into consideration, follow-up work can then be planned to consolidate and build on the training delivered. This provides good accountability evidence for senior managers and OFSTED, and demonstrates the school's (and SENCo's) effectiveness. Ideas for follow-up activities are suggested below.

- a regular 'surgery' where teachers and TAs can seek advice from the SENCo or speech and language therapist;
- optional 'advanced' CPD for interested staff;
- opportunities for teachers to observe intervention programmes – in their own school or elsewhere;
- a working party to trial a new approach or piece of new technology;
- an action-research project to test an intervention and report back to staff on its effectiveness;
- classroom observations by the SENCo to monitor colleagues' effectiveness in providing for the needs of children with cerebral palsy.

Section 10

Resources, acknowledgements and contacts

48 Resources to support pupils with cerebral palsy

Category	Item	Supplier
	PM starters reading books	Nelson Thornes
	Reading helper	Reading Helper Tel: 0113 257 7796
	Reading window/ruler	LDA, TTS
	Coloured overlays	TTS
	Sentence Builder app Part of a set of SALT apps	Mobile Education Store
	Sentence Maker app One of lots of good apps by this maker	Innovative Investments Limited
Language support	**Sound buttons/talking tins**	Widely available on the internet, try www.primary classroomresources.co.uk/ teaching
Maths	**Numicon**	Oxford University Press Amazon
	Special Numbers app for Apple devices	www.specialiapps.co.uk Appstore
	Match and Find app	www.specialiapps.co.uk

Resources to support fine motor development

Category	Item	Supplier
Fine motor skills box	Skill development	tts-group.co.uk
Scissors	Mounted table top scissors	Peta (UK) Ltd and tts-group.co.uk
	Pushdown table scissors	As above
	Dual control training scissors (L & R)	As above
	Mini easy grip (loop) scissors	As above
	Long loop scissors (L & R)	As above
	Self opening scissors	As above

Category	Item	Supplier
	Self opening long loop scissors	As above
	Comprehensive assessment kit	As above
	Fiskar Squeezers	NES Arnold
	Fiskar Junior scissors (L & R)	As above
	Fiskars for kids	As above
	Self-opening scissors (L & R)	Smith and Nephew, Homecraft
Developing cutting skills	'Programme to support cutting skills'	LDA
	'Developing Scissor Skills'	Peta (UK) Ltd
Pencil grips	Tri-go	Taskmaster Ltd
	Stubbi (same as Stetro)	As above
	Ultra grip	As above
	Comfort grip	As above
	Crossguard	As above
	Claw grip	As above
	Handi writer (puts pencil into web of hand)	Tts
Dycem	Non-slip material on roll	Patterson Medical
	Self-adhesive strips (to make non-slip rulers)	As above
Sloping writing surface	Write Angle	Completecareshop 0845 5194 734
	Writestart Desk	LDA
	Posture Pack	Back in Action Tel: 020 7930 8309
Pencils	Writestart pencils	Variety of sources on line
	Berol handhugger pencils	As above
	Noris Triplus Triangular pencils	As above
	S move pens and pencils (left handed and right handed)	www.stabilo.com or many stationers
Pens	Berol handhugger fibre tip pen	As above
	Rubber barrel pens with varying flow/resistance	Most stationery shops
Handwriting programmes	'Write from the Start' Book 1 and 2 by Teodorescu & L Addy	Available from Internet sources
Category	**Item**	**Supplier**
Compass	Safe drawing compass	Hope Education www.eaieducation.com

Rulers	Alligator easi grip ruler	NES Arnold, Taskmaster
	Make your own non-slip ruler using 2 × 1 cm strips of self-adhesive Dycem to the back of the ruler	
Construction toys	Stickle bricks	Yorkshire Purchasing Organisation
	Magnetic blocks	
	Clic	

Resources to support PE

Beanbags	Available as rabbits, frogs and turtles	NES Arnold
	Sensory ball pack	Yorkshire Purchasing
Balls	Spordas spider ball	NES Arnold
	Koosh ball	As above
	Tail ball	As above
	Floater ball (large, light slow moving)	As above
	Plus balls (inflatable paper balls – very slow)	As above
	Easy Katch ball (tendrils)	Hope Education
	Rubber flex Graballs	As above
	Bump ball (easy catch)	TTS Group
	Sure grip netball	TTS Group
	Play catch net	Cost Cutters educational suppliers
Group work equipment	Balance sets	Hope Education
	Agility ladder	TTS Group
	Tactile discs (stepping game)	TTS Group
Basketball	Adjustable height basketball net	As above
	Little Sure Shot	Hope Education

Resources to support food technology

Non-slip mats	Dycem mats available individually or on a roll	ROMPA 08452301177
Holding equipment	Clyde grater, scraper and spike – to hold vegetables, and integral grater on a non-slip base	Complete Care Shop 0845 194 734 www.nrshealthcare.co.uk
	Food preparation system – for use by those who have difficulties gripping	As above
	Pan handle holder – to prevent the pan moving while stirring with one hand	As above
	Kettle tilt – to assist with pouring	As above
Alternative cutting equipment	Rapid chopper – a single hand operated chopper with an integral blade	As above
Slide and hide oven		www.neff.co.uk
Perching stool	Height adjustable stool	www.nrshealthcare.co.uk

Resources to support recording skills

Spelling	Starspell (computer program)	Inclusive Technology
	'Toe by Toe' by Keda & Harry Cowling	Toe by Toe (ISBN 0952256401)
	Nessy	Inclusive Technology
Number	'Numbershark' (computer program)	Inclusive Technology
Recording	'Co:Writer' (word prediction)	Inclusive Technology
	Clicker software Clicker apps	Crick Software Ltd www.cricksoft.com.uk
	WriteOnline App	Crick software
	Dragon Naturally Speaking	www.shopnuance.co.uk/Dragon
	Penfriend	Inclusive Technology
	Special Stories	Special

ICT equipment

Keyboard letter stickers	Lower case stickers for younger pupils	Inclusive Technology
Big keys	Large keys (upper or lower case)	Inclusive Technology, SEMERC
Alternative mice	Roller balls etc	Inclusive Technology
Keyboards	Varied keyboards and keyguards	Inclusive Technology
Eyegaze		Inclusive Technology
Switches		Inclusive Technology

Publications

Teachers Standards, 2012	Department of Education	www.education.gov.uk/schools
Special Educational Needs and Disability Code of Practice, 2014	Department of Education	www.gov.uk
Supporting Pupils with a Medical Condition in School	Department of Education	www.gov.uk
Pivats		www.lancashire.gov.uk
Bsquared		www.bsquared.co.uk
CASPA		www.casponline.co.uk
Writing Handwriting	IPASS	01482 318400
Ready Steady…go to PE	IPASS	01482 318400

Contacts

www.scope.org.uk
www.cerebralpalsy.org.uk

References/further reading

Bailey, G. (2012) *Emotional Well-Being for Children with Special Educational Needs and Disabilities.* London: SAGE Publications Ltd.

Burrell, A. and Riley, J. (2005) *Promoting Children's Well-Being.* Stafford: Network Educational Press Ltd.

Edwards, M. and Titman, P. (2010) *Promoting Psychological Well-Being in Children with Acute and Chronic Illness.* London: Jessica Kingsley Publishers.

Appendices

Appendix 1 Some professionals who may be involved with the pupil

Professional	Personnel and contact number
Educational psychologist	
Specialist Teaching Service for Physical Disability	
Speech and language therapist	
Visual Impairment Service	
Hearing Impairment Service	
School nurse	
Physiotherapist	
Occupational therapist	
Orthotics	
Wheelchair services	
Social care	

Appendix 2   Basic document requirements for disabled children and young people

These documents should be in place (where relevant).

1	PEEP – Personal Emergency Evacuation Plan	Yes ☐	No ☐
2	IHCP – Individual Health Care Plan	Yes ☐	No ☐
3	ICP – Intimate Care Plan	Yes ☐	No ☐
4	Handling Plan – Assisted Transfers Risk Assessments i.e. OT plans, physiotherapy plans – kept up to date	Yes ☐	No ☐
5	Hoisting Recommendation/Guidance – relevant documentation re: training	Yes ☐	No ☐
6	**PUWER** (Provision and Usage of Work Equipment Regulations) **LOLER** (Lifting Operations and Lifting Equipment Regulations) – Equipment checks and inspections – 6 monthly documents to evidence. Plinths, Hoist, Slings.	Yes ☐	No ☐
7	W/C Proficiency Test, guidance of electric chairs around school for staff. Insurance – whom does it cover?	Yes ☐	No ☐
8	Swimming Risk Assessments	Yes ☐	No ☐
9	Educational Visits Risk Assessment	Yes ☐	No ☐

These are all highly recommended documents that may also be requested during OFSTED inspections.

(With thanks to IPaSS Hull.)

Appendix 3 Transition planning

Planning for transition	Action required
Staff involved	
Funding	
Staff involved in transition: early years setting/primary and secondary schools Parents and pupil Specialist Teaching Service for Physical Disability Speech and language therapist Occupational therapist Physiotherapist	
Training delivered by: Specialist Teaching Service for Physical Disability Speech and language therapist Occupational therapist Physiotherapist	
Access audit made	
Manual handling training given	
Mobility around school, support required	
Specialist seating requirements	
Communication passport in place	
Access to curriculum	
ICT requirements identified	
Fire evacuation plans in place	
Toileting requirements, Intimate hygiene plan in place	
Medical needs identified	

Child protection issues	
Lunchtime plans	
After-school clubs	
Transport to and from school	
Home/school liaison	

Appendix 4　Personal Emergency Evacuation Plan (PEEP)

Directorate/Service	

Name	
Site	
Rooms/areas/floors used within school	
Name of manager responsible for PEEP	
Telephone No. and extension	
Date of PEEP assessment	

REASON FOR PEEP

MOBILITY ISSUES

- ☐ Unable to walk
- ☐ Cannot transfer/move easily
- ☐ Unable to use stairs
- ☐ Can only use stairs with assistance
- ☐ Temporary issues, e.g. broken leg
- ☐ Use of a wheelchair
- ☐ Use of electric wheelchair
- ☐ Uses walking aid

EMOTIONAL ISSUES

- ☐ _____

LEARNING DISABILITIES

- ☐ _____

OTHER HEALTH ISSUES

- ☐ Asthma
- ☐ Epilepsy
- ☐ Dyslexia
- ☐ Dexterity problems
- ☐ Orientation disorder
- ☐ Temporary, e.g. broken arm

NORMAL SUPPORT REQUIRED
(Link to Care Plan if appropriate)

PROCEDURE IN THE EVENT OF AN EMERGENCY

METHOD OF ASSISTANCE
(e.g. transfer procedures, methods of guidance, etc.)

☐   Use of an evacuation chair

☐   Can get downstairs using handrails

☐   Needs assistance with 1 person

☐   Needs assistance with 2 persons

☐   Can move down stairs on their bottom

☐   Needs doors opening

☐   Provision of audible alarms

☐   Use of buddy system

☐   Provision of additional handrails

☐   Provision of push bars/pads to doors

☐   Needs familiarisation with fire exits/escape routes

Add any others

EQUIPMENT PROVIDED:

EGRESS PROCEDURE: (A step-by-step account beginning from the first alarm)

SAFE ROUTES:

DESIGNATED ASSISTANCE
Give names of staff
'The following people have been designated to give assistance out of the building in an emergency.'

COMMUNICATION
State how this information has been communicated to individuals/staff/carers/parents/fire wardens/nominated 'buddies' etc.

ACTION PLAN – Add more rows if necessary
Ensure Care Plan is updated/amended if appropriate

No	ACTION	TO BE COMPLETED BY		ACTION COMPLETE	
		NAME	DATE	NAME	DATE
1					
2					
3					
4					
5					
6					
7					
8					
9					
10					

AWARENESS OF PROCEDURE

I have received the evacuation procedure in the following format:

☐   The evacuation routes have been explained to me

☐   The evacuation routes have been shown to me

☐   I have my own authorised plan

I am informed of an emergency evacuation by:

☐   Existing fire system

☐   Members of my work team (each of these require a copy of this PEEP)

☐   The fire wardens on my floor (each of these require a copy of this PEEP)

☐   Other (please specify)

'I have been fully involved in the production of this PEEP and I am aware of the procedure to be followed in the event of an emergency evacuation. I will inform my manager if my condition changes which will affect it.'	Signature of individual (if appropriate)

MANAGER SIGNATURE	
'This PEEP has been carried out in conjunction with the individual (where appropriate) and has been formally communicated as above.'	Signature of manager

Scheduled date of next review	Any changes in condition or location? Clarify that all controls are still in place	Signature of manager	Date of review

Schedule the review of the Peep in line with the Care Plan Review (if appropriate)

The above form is from IPaSS (Integrated Physical and Sensory Services), Hull.

Appendix 5 Points to consider when planning and risk assessing swimming lessons for a child with a physical disability

Pupil's name: …………………………….. DOB: ………………………..

What are the pupil's main additional needs? Outline briefly and specify any moving and handling equipment used in school:

……………………………………………………………………………………………………

……………………………………………………………………………………………………

☐ Cerebral palsy

☐ Mobility

☐ Hand skills

☐ Communication

☐ Incontinence issues

☐ Concentration difficulties

☐ Epilepsy*

☐ Diabetes* (food/drink supply permitted on poolside)

☐ Asthma – inhaler to go onto poolside

*Written medical approval must be provided by parents/guardians to accompany the Advance Notice Form – a copy must be provided to the swimming teacher at start of the 1st lesson.

Does the child go swimming with the family?	☐ yes ☐ no
	If yes….
	☐ weekly
	☐ monthly
	☐ during family holidays

How would the parents describe their child's attitude to swimming?	☐ do not know ☐ confident ☐ nervous
Do the parents use any special approaches?	☐ buoyancy aids (specify) ☐ only swims on back due to physical disability
What type of seating will the child use on the bus?	☐ standard seat with seat belt ☐ manual wheelchair
Will you need to allocate additional staff for the journey?	• the driver will be responsible for loading, clamping and offloading wheelchair users
Are staff familiar with the route from the bus car park to the wheelchair accessible entrance?	• pre-visit advisable • request that wheelchair user is off loaded first to allow maximum time for changing
Are staff familiar with the location of the accessible changing area?	• pre-visit advisable
Does the changing area have all the moving and handling equipment that the child normally uses? If not, what is your contingency plan?	☐ grab rails ☐ height adjustable changing bed ☐ hoist (take own sling if required)
When and where will staff change?	• suggest they go with swimwear under their clothing • staff (and children) are permitted to wear suitable clothing other than swim wear e.g. shorts and tee-shirts
Who will help the child change? Request that swim wear is worn under the child's clothing.	1 2 3 (reserve in case of absence)
If the child is bowel incontinent it is the parent/carers responsibility to provide protective swimwear.	For examples of suitable items see http://www.incywincy.net
What position will the child get changed in?	☐ standing ☐ sitting in wheelchair ☐ lying on the changing bed
How will the child move to the poolside?	☐ Walk – unaided, with oversight, with assistance ☐ manual wheelchair ☐ pool chair

How will you minimise risk of injury to staff?	• ensure staff work in accordance with moving and handling guidance • remove all jewellery before leaving school • wear covered footwear, e.g. trainers when working with a child in a wheelchair • follow the physiotherapist's moving and handling guidance provided for toileting and transfer routines in school
How many staff will be needed to get the child in the water?	• are staff trained in moving and handling? • are they familiar with working with the child?
It is a school responsibility to provide support staff to enter the water. Who will support the child in the water? Will you have a substitute in case of absence or fatigue?	• responsible adult required in the water to support children with a significant physical disability, e.g. unable to walk independently • 1:1 spotter required for children who have 1:1 SEN support in school • 1:1 spotter required for children with epilepsy • responsible adult required in the water if child with epilepsy is out of depth
How will the child get in and out the water? • ask advice of physiotherapist/ moving and handling trainer • arrange pre-visit with child and above personnel if necessary	☐ enter via steps as other children independently ☐ enter via step with adult support ☐ enter from sitting position on side and be received by adult in pool ☐ enter via pool hoist and be received by adult in pool
Are any emergency evacuation procedures required? **Not usually – pool staff are trained in evacuation of disabled swimmers**	• inform pool manager of the child's disability or medical condition and ask if they require additional training for emergency evacuation of this child • liaise with moving and handling trainer if required
How will the child exit the pool?	☐ using same method as when entering pool ☐ as advised by moving and handling trainer/physiotherapist
How will the child move to the changing area? Note: Only wheelchairs with vinyl upholstery protected by towels can be used when the child is wet	☐ walk – unaided, with oversight, with assistance ☐ manual wheelchair ☐ pool chair

When and where will staff change?	• suggest staff wear towelling dressing gowns whilst child is dried and dressed • hand child over to supervising teacher whilst support staff dry and dress

Who can you contact for further advice?

Transport

School visits advisor

Swimming lesson co-ordinator

Physiotherapy service

Moving and Handling Trainer

Support teacher

Appendix 6 Pro forma for Intimate Care Plan

Name of pupil	
Date of birth	
Address	
Name of parent/carer/guardian	Name of staff
Contact number	
Date written	Review date
Pupil's condition	
Where the intimate care procedure will take place	
How the pupil will travel there, e.g. walk, wheelchair – self propel/adult oversight	
What equipment is required and where located	
Description of transfer method	
Adjustment of clothing	
Method of cleansing, including washing hands	
Appropriate language, e.g. names for body parts and functions	
Number of staff, i.e. one or two	
Pupil participation, i.e. what can they do	
Disposal	
Next target towards independence	
Signature of parent/carer/guardian	Signature/s of staff involved with procedure/s

Appendix 7 Pro forma for an Individual Health Care Plan

Individual Health Care Plans should not be onerous but capture key information necessary to maintain the pupil's well being. The complexity of the plan will depend on the severity of the pupil's needs. The plan should be available to everyone involved in the pupil's care but confidentiality should also be observed. Where the pupil has a special educational need described in a statement or EHC plan the IHCP should be linked or be part of either.

Schools should make their own decisions about the format of their Individual Health Care Plan, however, the following is a pro forma from Supporting Pupils with a Medical Condition in School, 2014:

Name of school/setting	
Child's name	
Group/class/form	
Date of birth	
Child's address	
Medical diagnosis or condition	
Date	
Review date	

Family Contact Information

Name	
Phone no. (work)	
(home)	
(mobile)	
Name	
Relationship to child	
Phone no. (work)	
(home)	
(mobile)	

Clinic/Hospital Contact

Name

Phone no.

GP

Name

Phone no.

Who is responsible for providing support in school

Describe medical needs and give details of child's symptoms, triggers, signs, treatments, facilities, equipment or devices, environmental issues, etc.

Name of medication, dose, method of administration, when to be taken, side effects, contra-indications, administered by/self-administered with/without supervision

Daily care requirements

Specific support for the pupil's educational, social and emotional needs

Arrangements for school visits/trips etc

Other information

Describe what constitutes an emergency, and the action to take if this occurs

Who is responsible in an emergency *(state if different for off-site activities)*

```
```

Plan developed with

```
```

Staff training needed/undertaken – who, what, when, how often it should be renewed

```
```

Form copied to

```
```